MW01196477

PRAISE FOR "EMBARRASSING CONFESSIONS OF A MARINE LIEUTENANT" FROM THE PEOPLE THESE BOOKS SHOULD BE WRITTEN FOR-ENLISTED MARINES, SOLDIERS, AND SAILORS

"Greatest fuckin work of literature ever produced. I laughed harder at the preface than I have in the 2 years I've been out. This book is a great pick me up with a serious message. It shows me I'm not alone in the world and I'm not the only one who thinks and acts like I do. Like a Marine! Keep up the good work!"   - Enlisted Marine

"I would recommend this to my entire Family....and I think this sums up the irreverence and humor you need to process the things you need to do in combat and bring everyone home! It has always been hard to describe my experiences to someone that hasn't "Been There." I know I had a long transition back to relative normalcy (still a ways to go)."
– Enlisted Soldier

"I almost wanted to re-enlist after reading this" – Enlisted Marine

"As much as I want to say 'don't read this book,' O'Malley's willingness to expose the male brain at war, with pure, unadulterated honesty shrouded in explicit sexual delusion gives Embarrassing Confessions of A Marine Officer a unique and never before reading experience or perspective for the reader. It is a 'first of its' kind' and I think, albeit, complicit and entirely inappropriate as a whole, O'Malley's end goal of helping those who have suffered the ugliness of war and subsequent suicide causalities, can and will benefit from the humor he intended his readers to enjoy through his complete transparency. He is a pioneer of sorts into the land of veteran suicides in his attempt to bring awareness and help to those in need. So for that reason, I can stand behind his first published achievement. I will also add that the "gay chicken" chapter had me laugh out loud several times and let it be noted that I found the need for male affection and companionship in such grisly environments somewhat tender and enduring. I'm looking forward to reading his blog and contributing to his organization." – Cool Civilian

"Thanks for the laughs. Screw you for making me remember that we were F'd up all the way back to Vietnam."
– Enlisted Marine

"If Generation Kill had been written by Sterling Archer. Anyone who's a fan of the show "Archer" will know what I mean. Those who have served as a combat Soldier or Marine will (at least privately) acknowledge that this work is in many ways a refraction of our own deployments. This is easily the only book on modern warfare in existence that is completely raw and open about the types of twisted thoughts that go through the minds of those asked to do the insane, under asinine conditions, while trying to keep from going completely mad. I read this in a single afternoon, and only momentarily paused from laughing my backside off, as Capt O'Malley punctuates each chapter with the name of a Marine who committed suicide. Having recently lost my best friend (a fellow Soldier) to suicide, this

resonated   with   me.
Those looking for a book on self-righteous heroism, or "patriotic" garble that will somehow justify what we had to do, look elsewhere. Rather, this is an expose on all of the gritty, raw, inappropriate, and downright raunchy thoughts that went through our minds constantly, yet we're too embarrassed to admit. Make no mistake, this book is extremely vulgar and will doubtless make many uncomfortable. It is also a quick read, which I breezed through in a few hours, while all-the-while hearing the story told through Sterling Archer's voice in my head. The story is less of a narrative about a combat mission in Afghanistan, but rather a confession of every embarrassing thought and action, told in sordid detail, that will resonate with most combat veterans. Part of the appeal is that it comes from an officer, proving that they are human (and in many ways just as or more jacked
up) like the rest of us."   – Enlisted Marine

"I admire the bravery to put aside political correctness, and to shed light on a disgusting issue arising in our generation of Marines. This book captivates its veteran audience by nostalgia, and its civilian audience by, presumably nausea. Thanks." – Enlisted Marine

"This is the real deal, and O'Malley is the platoon leader every grunt wants to have. He's the natural leader the brass hates, but the first one they look to when the shit hits the fan. As funny as it is, the ugly truth of suicide among combat vets comes through in a very sobering way. Thanks, "Lt. Dan", for holding the flank." – Enlisted Soldier

"Outstanding book. As a former Marine Sergeant from over 30 years ago. I laughed and chuckled all the way through the book. Capt. O'Malley really brought back some memories of crazy stuff we pulled. Should be a must read for all new Lt's in TBS...won't ever happen unfortunately. Officers need to learn and remember their main job is to take care of your Marines. They will make you a rock star and kill lots of turds."
– Enlisted Marine

"This book is hands down one the best I have ever read regarding life in the Marine Corps, Combat, and Afghanistan. I laughed so hard it hurt on many occasions, and above all, this book is going to save lives. 22 US veterans a day kill themselves due to PTSD related issues. The author issues several calls to action for the reader, and the country, to work against this... There is NO doubt in my mind this book will save lives. If you are a veteran, know a veteran, are interested in war, combat, the Marine Corps, the military, or especially are a guy with combat experience, this book will change your life. Huge thanks to the Author for this work." – Enlisted Marine

"This book was effing hilarious and I even woke up the wife a few times. This is the perfect insight into the mind of a Marine. It's not all chess and fighting lava beasts! The memorial pages are very poignant and the "orders" are so damn funny. On a serious note, I'm a USMC vet and have had some mental health issues not related to combat and on the day I read this book, I was on a bit of a downward swing. After reading it though, my mood was immediately lifted which I think was the intent of Donny's book." – Enlisted Marine

"Mr. O'Malley does a fantastic job mixing in some honest to goodness humor to get this point across. I have absolutely no doubt that serving under Mr. O'Malley was indeed an experience of a lifetime. As a prior enlisted man, I would have been honored to go into battle with him because of his down-to-earth leadership style. I guarantee you Mr. O'Malley had the respect of his men. For most of the book, Mr. O'Malley uses sexually graphic self-deprecating humor to get across his real message -- at least 22 veterans commit suicide everyday."
– Enlisted Sailor

"This book is an excellent window into the mind of a male in a combat zone. True, gritty, raw and hilarious. If you have ever been lucky enough to enjoy the thrills of a sexually deprived combat zone, this book will bring back memories of smashing off knuckle babies in a plywood Porta John and playing spades and gay chicken in between firefights. This book is like herpes, once you've read it you can't unread the stories and it sticks with you. Be a bro and give it to someone you love, or just want to hook up with for the night. On a serious note, it also brings to light the very real problem of veteran suicide and presents a simple and realistic solution to the problem. Hopefully the right person reads through this book and puts this plan into action."   – Enlisted Marine

"Your book does something that I've never seen another book do before: it takes a look inside the mind of someone who's actually been there honestly. We don't always think about some noble Bing West/Jim Webb stuff. Sometimes we play the "beat off or pass out in the porta john" game. We are not our father's generation, when killing was seen as the anti-thesis of humanity. We truly are Generation Kill, and this book takes the most unfiltered, truthful, straightforward look at the actually thoughts of a grunt-a boots on the ground grunt- that I have ever read. Not only is it the most honest account that I've read this far in my life, but the style makes you forget about the horrible reality of war with its irreverent take on things. And THAT's how the mind of a grunt functions. We have to find the humor during war, or we might go nuts. Gay chicken is something I've never seen addressed in any other book, but it's an infantry staple. If you can't hang, if you can't get at least a little gay, you might be too uptight to fight a war. We all get gay and shit because of the close bonds we form, and our love of one another. As the Dominican grunt said to you, Donny, you get infantry Marines on a level no other officer does, or maybe would admit to."

–Enlisted Marine

"Donny O'Malley says what many officers think, but don't say (out loud). His deviant behavior and lack of decency gave me some of the most side-splitting fits of laughter in my life. And as a someone who has served (and continues to serve) through four combat deployments, I understand the importance of laughter during shared misery. His words will make you recoil in disgust, laugh your ass off, and give you a newfound respect for the men and women who put life and limb on the line. Contrary to what some will say, this book is a life line to all service members everywhere suffering through wounds seen and unseen... As well as closeted, degenerate officers. Thanks Donny!"   – Cool Marine Officer

"I found his book base, vulgar, and disgusting......There's a huge difference between 'swears like a sailor' and the bile that spews from his mouth. His propensity for sexual depravity, acts, feelings about killing, and women borders on sociopathy."
– Nerdy Marine Officer who never left the wire.

EMBARRASSING CONFESSIONS OF A MARINE LIEUTENANT

OPERATION BRANDING IRON: PART 2.1A

BY DONNY O'MALLEY

Irreverent

ir·rev·er·ent

əˈrev(ə)rənt/

adjective

1. showing a lack of respect for people or things that are generally taken seriously.

2. deficient in veneration or respect

3. an inability to take serious things seriously

Made in the United States of America
This book represents my experiences as I remember
them. If there are any inaccuracies in my stories, I *want*
to correct them, so please email me. And no, you cannot
correct my thoughts, they will always be wrong and the
world is better off that way, so don't ask.

I changed some names and situations in an attempt to
leave some peoples dignity intact.

O'Malley Entertainment, LLC
ISBN-10: 1943979006
ISBN-13: 978-1-943979-00-4
Copyright © 2015 Danny Maher

Front cover photo taken by Josh Brown
Edited by Aaron Moshier

Rear cover photo taken by Aaron Moshier
Edited by Aaron Moshier

Table of Contents

DEDICATION

This book is dedicated to every man, dead or alive, who signed up to hunt and kill the enemies of the United States before they killed us. You great men made an incredible sacrifice of limb, life, and mind that will never be forgotten.

PREFACE

Until I went to combat, making my buddies laugh excited me more than anything else in life. (Well, that's not entirely true. Before combat, nothing has ever excited me more than a fully conscious woman who's willing to sleep with me.)

Once I got to combat and experienced killing other men who Uncle Sam and I both deemed to be pieces of shit, comedy became a fun way to deal with watching human beings get maimed, and killing became the most exciting thing in life. (Killing vs. Pussy..... still a toss up)

After returning home from combat the Marine Corps put me in Wounded Warrior Battalion and began the medical separation process. (I wasn't hit by enemy fire, I'm just a pussy made of brittle glass.) Once I knew that my war fighting days were over I fell back on my old passion: comedy. I spent my free time, laid up on the couch, turning all my old journal entries and crazy experiences into decently written stories with the intention of publishing a bunch of books. I wasn't sure what the books would be, nor in what order; I just knew I would write books and make people laugh.

It was obvious from day one that my military stories were my best stories, but I was so depressed about not being in the Infantry anymore that I avoided anything military; including military movies, books, and especially, writing my own military stories. Instead I wrote my old college frat partying stories, usually involving booze, sex, and fighting. I tried not to think nor write about the Marine Corps Infantry, because the Infantry—the one true love of my life—was gone.

While I was laid up post surgery, writing my childish stories of partying, a weird thing started happening. Friends of friends started killing themselves— and they were all combat vets who'd been to the area I was in. Thanks to the surgery I was constantly fucked up on narcotics, plus I didn't know any of these guys- so it didn't hit me hard, it just made me wonder.

What the fuck is goin' on?

I became compelled to nut up and write my Marine Corps stories.

As I rewrote my old Marine Corps stories and journal entries I quickly realized they were horribly inappropriate for any normal person, but were far less appropriate for a Marine Captain. So like a pussy, not wanting to be criticized, I watered my stories down to make them less offensive, childish, and unprofessional.

That made me a fucking phony.

The truth, validated by everyone who has ever known me, is that my sense of humor is terribly offensive, my personality is embarrassingly childish, and when I tell of a group of guys a story, I am the polar opposite of professional.

While in Wounded Warrior Battalion I made friends with a guy named Art Lazukin. Art was a rifleman in First Battalion Fifth Marine Regiment when he lost his legs to an IED in Sangin, and like me, was being medically retired. I sent him the link to a few of the raw and unprofessional stories on my website, and two weeks later he texted me with the most meaningful compliment and influential advice anyone has ever given me.

"Dude, as soon as I feel a glimpse of sadness I go on your website. I've been rereading it and it's the only thing that makes me laugh hysterically. Can't thank you enough bro, you're doing God's work. Thanks once again bro. Keep being raw and honest, fuck what anyone says, and no matter what DON'T EVER STOP BEING YOURSELF."

I took his advice to heart, and decided that I wasn't being honest enough in most of my writing. I realized that I had changed my thoughts to be less offensive because I didn't want people to judge me.

So I went back and took the water out of my stories. I made the dialogue more raw and realistic, I wrote about more embarrassing things I'd done, and I included more of my own vile thoughts, all of which I was initially afraid to publish.

The results of my changes are the most politically incorrect, inappropriate, unprofessional, and embarrassing stories about war that have ever been written. The things I say in this book should not be written by any man, let alone a Marine officer.

Every senior officer who reads this will slam me, military historians will be shocked, and normal, good-hearted American citizens will look at me like I'm a sociopath.

Making this more exciting for me, is that I don't give one flying fuck what *they* think, because when it comes to the opinions of anyone who is not a door kicking, minesweeping, chain smoking, "RipIt" chugging, gun wielding, body slaying, combat veteran; I give ZERO FUCKS.

After all, I'm not writing for *them*. Every war book ever written, was written for *them*. Not a single war book has ever been written specifically for enlisted warriors, without regard for what anyone else thinks, until now.

I write for enlisted Marines, Sailors, and Soldiers.

You are the reason I served, *you* are the one I stole food from the Officer's mess for, *you* are the one I gave the shirt off my back to, *you* are the reason I argued with my Company Commanders and almost came to blows, *you* are the reason I disobeyed orders, *you* are the reason I loved every second of every day I spent as a Marine, and *you* are the reason I write today.

I write because I want your attention.

I want your attention because our nation's combat veterans are blowing their own brains out at a rate that is hard to comprehend. When combat veterans get out of the military and lose the brotherhood that has supported them for years, their life gets very lonely, and very dark. The demonic parasites that have lived inside them since going to combat will eat at them every day until they finally decide the only way to kill the demon is to kill the host.

As combat veterans, we have to be there for each other, every day, until the day we die: even if it's just to share a laugh, or share a nightmare.

We must stick together. Civilians cannot help us, only we can help each other.

Remember my friend Art? The guy who is most responsible for the honesty in my writing?

He fed himself a bullet on March 29, 2015. He was so goddamned caring and considerate that he used a pillow to silence the pistol and minimize splatter. He was just that kind of guy.

He was one of way *more* than 22 veterans who killed themselves that day.

I don't have the answers, I just have the ability to make people laugh and bring people together, and that's what I want to do with this book.

I'm writing this book not only to entertain, but to provide therapy to veterans who feel that no one understands them. To veterans who are angry about what they had to do, think, and see. To veterans who believed whole-heartedly in the intentions and competency of the United States of America and our military leadership, and at some point felt let down.

To veterans who ever asked the question, "what the fuck are we doing here?" To veterans who lost limbs, eyes, minds, and friends while fighting to take ground in Iraq and Afghanistan, who now get to watch as the Taliban and ISIS take that ground back. To veterans who can't help but wonder if everything we did over there was a fucking waste. To veterans who came back from the shithole that is the middle-east, to an American population who loved them, but couldn't understand them.

I want this book to provide therapy, promote understanding, and restore faith.

I will write the things that every combat veteran was and still is thinking, but never had the balls to say in public- and then I'm going to make a joke about them.

Humor is the way I deal with anything that sucks. I can dwell on anger and sadness if I choose. I can hate my government for sending us to impose democracy on a culture that's not built to embrace it, I can hate my bosses for imposing ridiculous rules of engagement on me. I can be angry at the Afghan people for being such pieces of shit and not taking control of their own country. I can allow myself to stay full of anger and hate, or I can make a joke, let go, and press on. I CHOOSE to joke, because it's better than the alternative.

In combat- in a lifestyle of constant discomfort, fear, trauma, and tragedy- humor is the preferred method of coping.

If we allowed ourselves to wallow on our discomforts, pains, and fears, we'd never be effective in combat. Therefore those negative emotions must get tossed to the wayside.

All that's left is laughter, and love for each other.

Most of the men I served with in the military used humor to deal with everything that sucked, and as I now deal with my fellow veterans killing themselves at a rate of far more than 22 per day, I continue to use humor.

This book is a collection of TRUE stories and ACTUAL journal entries from combat. Every story started as a journal entry written while I was in Shitghanistan. The most deserving journal entries were rewritten into short stories, but I felt that some of the journal entries would be more powerful if I left them unedited.

I express my honest thoughts and actions about the way I approached and executed the last and most dangerous combat operation of my deployment. It was a nighttime helicopter raid into a Taliban controlled area. It was called Operation Branding Iron Part 2.1A, and I couldn't stop behaving like a horny, 16 year old girl going to prom.

I want this book to mirror the same emotional roller coaster that a warrior experiences in combat. Seriousness, fear, fun, humor, thrill, excitement, heartbreak, fear, seriousness, and
then right back to humor, fun, and thrill.
Between each chapter is the name of a warrior who has killed himself, at which time, I expect you to follow my call to action. It will suck for a quick second, but we'll get right   back   to   the   fun.

I have included the first story about my travel to Shitghanistan simply to introduce my sense of humor and make sure you don't ever make the mistake of taking me too seriously; the rest of the book is about the comedy, hunting, killing, and frustration surrounding Operation Branding Iron Part 2.1A.

Like I said, I don't have the answers, I just have the ability to make people laugh and bring people together.

Let's have a laugh at my expense, and then get together to stop these fucking suicides.

Warning:

If you're a pussy, if you think you know how warriors should behave without being a warrior yourself, or are easily offended, I don't want your money, so put this book down now and ask for a refund, because it is not for you. If you do decide to turn the page after this warning, do so with the understanding you're never going to look at a Marine Corps recruiting commercial the same again, because you'll know how disgusting we really are, and how disgusting we **need** to be in order to laugh as we maim other human beings and then step on their skulls.

Oh, and then come back into society and expect to be normal. Yeah, that's a fuckin' joke.

To everyone else, enjoy the show.

Disrespectfully,

"Donny O'Malley," Captain, USMC (ret.)

INTRODUCTION, TO ME

"My masseuse was not the slightest bit attractive, although it's hard to say for sure. Every guy knows that for 10 minutes after jerking off, nothing in the world is attractive. All sexual objectivity normally assumed by women is gone, and they are reduced to being actual people; with feelings, hopes, dreams, and even families who love them. So who knows? My masseuse could have been hot...I just wasn't in a position to judge."

Desperation can make a person do incredible things: Incredibly stupid things, incredibly sad things, incredibly terrible things, and incredibly shameful things. When I get desperate, I am capable of everything. This is a tale of one Marine's desperation as he headed into combat with a loaded gun.

The Road to War

March 1, 2012
Manas Air Force Base, Kyrgyzstan

Getting from the United States to Afghanistan was borderline unbearable. First, we boarded a miserable Delta 747, and as expected, I got screwed with the aisle seat in first class. The flight was an arduous 18 hours, and I was only able to get good sleep for 14 of them. For the few minutes I was awake, I was very disappointed with the movie selection on my personal television. Additionally, on every single one of the six meals we were served, my fucking bread was cold. This was not the glamorous way I expected to head into combat, but I was a Marine, and I could handle anything. So I walked out of first class, where they *didn't* serve us booze, and exited the airplane in Kyrgyzstan.

We crowded onto the flight line where it was 15 degrees. Then we piled way too many Marines into piece-of-shit buses that were so weighed down the bottom was scraping against the ground. We drove out of the airport and through a dark, rusty town that made me feel like we were in either a James Bond or WWII movie. Thanks to the clouds, snow, cold air, barbed wire fences and dying trees, it had a very Soviet, Cold War feel to it. My initial impression of historic shame was reaffirmed when a Marine started doing impressions of a Nazi soldier herding Jews. The Marine, a Jew *himself*, was yelling for the whole bus to hear, making it more outrageous.

"VOMEN and CHEELDREN, line TO ZE RIGHT. ABLE BODIED MEN, line TO ZE LEFT. Elderly and sickly, move quickly to ze showvas, we must get you clean IMMEDIATELY!"

The whole bus laughed hysterically; mostly because no one could believe a Jew would make that joke. One Marine on the back of the bus, who didn't know the Jew Marine yelled out,

"MY FUCKING FAMILY WAS KILLED IN THE HOLOCAUST MOTHERFUCKER. SHUT THE FUCK UP!"

The Jew Joker yelled back, "SO DID MINE BITCH, AND

THEY ALL HAD A SICK SENSE OF HUMOR, SO GET OVER IT."

The angry Marine looked confused and then settled back into his seat. There was some laughter and discussion as the Marine in the back pondered the sanity of the Marine Corps.

Our buses dropped us off on the front line of Manas Air Force Base: a huge transient base, first built as an airstrip for shuttling cargo into Afghanistan. It then became the stopping off point for troops heading into, and out of, Afghanistan. The base is outstanding, situated on flat ground and surrounded by beautiful mountains. It has three chow halls- all of which are amazing. It has a sports bar, a supermarket, a library with internet access, a huge gym with a basketball court, another brand new, state-of-the-art basketball court with six NBA regulation hoops in a large tent (the Air Force has a lot of black guys), volleyball courts, running paths, an entertainment club with TVs for movies, video games, and WI-FI. The place is just fantastic. I spent my entire time in Manas eating, sleeping, working out, and on the Internet. Like a real Marine.

There was also a big shopping center located on the base, with a nail salon (for all the fat, disgusting Air Force females), an alteration shop (for all the Airmen who gain 30 pounds while stationed there), a gear store (for all the Airmen to post pictures on Facebook holding knives and pretending to be badasses), a souvenir shop (so Airmen can prove to their families that they were deployed to a foreign country), and a massage parlor (because Airmen do hard, back breaking work.)

Naturally, I found my way to the massage parlor. It served two purposes for me: first, ever since I injured my back on my first deployment, I have needed massages at least monthly to be able to turn my head properly without lots of painkillers. Second, I desperately wanted to feel a woman's hands on me. I had not been with a woman in a whole five days, and I was desperately craving a woman's touch. A back massage was a great start, but I was really hoping that the massages came with happy endings. In Thailand, you couldn't go anywhere without women begging to tug on your dick for a few bucks, so naturally, I figured that every woman in a foreign country working on a United States military base had an entrepreneurial spirit and a knack for stroking cocks. Besides, to any deployed Marine, the words "Massage Parlor" are synonymous with "Happy Ending."

As I walked up to the massage parlor door, I had a quick fantasy of a small, smooth hand with nice nails wrapped around my dick (quite frankly, my big, calloused hand was getting old). As a matter of fact, I really didn't care if the masseuses were hideous. Hell, I didn't even care if their hands were bigger than mine. Truth be told, I just wanted a female's hand around my dick, and I wanted to blow a load that at least partially landed on female skin (blowing loads into porta potties and napkins was getting old too).

I was well aware that if I got a hand job with my massage, I was more than likely going to blow my load on *myself*. But I imagined that if just one, tiny, drop of jizz got on my masseuses hand, or forearm or, God willing, her tits, I could sleep easy at night knowing that I served the needs of the Marine Corps, and all mankind.

All my fantasizing was very preemptive, because there was really a 50/50 chance that the massage parlor gave out happy endings. I had no way to know until I was lying on the massage table; all I had was hope, and God's will. Inshallah.

By the time I got into the massage parlor, I had been in Kyrgyzstan, searching for halfway decent looking females, for approximately 6 hours. Despite my impressively low standards, (thanks to my ability to see beauty on a deep level) I still didn't see any good looking locals, so I was starting to worry about the quality of the masseuses.

All the women from Kyrgyzstan were unlike any women I had ever seen. They looked like a mixture of Russians, Middle Easterners, and Asians, and they all spoke with Russian accents. Soon after arriving in Manas, I learned that good ole' Genghis Khan had raped and pillaged his way through Kyrgyzstan 800 years prior; thereby adding superior mathematical ability, tight pussies, and little dicks into the bloodline.

I thought about the way they fought wars back then. I highly doubted that Genghis Khan's campaign across Eurasia was hindered by rules of engagement and rules of war. I can only imagine how much fun and how little stress those guys had in combat. But I digress....

I stepped into the massage parlor and saw, to my immediate right, four fat Airmen and four Infantry Marines. The Airmen looked relaxed, but the Marines looked both excited and uneasy. They looked like they were excited at the idea that they might possibly get a happy ending, but weren't sure about how to ask. I could relate to them. Right above their heads, on the wall, was a large sign that read, "IT IS AGAINST THE LAW TO SOLICIT SEXUAL ACTS." This explained why they looked uneasy.

To my front and left were the curtains separating the massage rooms and the masseuses. Within less than one second, I was finished with a scan of five women, and I realized that I'd have to drink about 17 beers to fuck any of them. I was like the Terminator in the opening scene of T2, when he walked into the bar and began scanning people—except my brain worked much faster than his processor, and it was only concerned with assessing "fuckability." When I made eye contact with the masseuses, I got the impression they were very attracted to me. I could see the thick, curly hair stand up on the back of their necks, I sensed their insatiable thirst for my dick, and I saw a quick scene of me fucking all five of them at once, with an empty 20-rack on the floor.
The way my brain works when I'm horny is truly incredible.

Seeing how excited these women were at the sight of my charming smile and buff American body, instantly turned them from 4s into 5s. Any woman willing to fuck me becomes magically more attractive. It's like a gift I have. I make women prettier with my presence, because I am selfless and kind.

I flirted with the Mongol-Russian hybrid working the front desk while four other women looked me up and down, imagining what it would be like to massage me. I felt very attractive at that moment. I put my name down for a massage the next afternoon, gave the front desk girl a wink, and took a deep breath through my nostrils; as expected, I could smell her sopping wet crotch as it yearned for me. I walked back to my barracks feeling like a million bucks; full of excitement, and myself.

I spent the rest of the night on Facebook like a loser, and sleeping like a leader.

When I woke up at 11AM the next morning, two of the other platoon commanders from Fox Company, Toby and Boden, were just getting back home from the massage parlor. They were excited to tell me about their experiences getting massaged.

Boden was the first to speak.

"Donny, wake the fuck up man! You gotta hear about the massage parlor."

I felt my dick move. I immediately assumed that he got a hand job, which confirmed my hopes that the sign about 'not soliciting sexual acts' was bullshit. I sat up quickly and said,

"Pleeeeeease tell me you got a hand job," my face looked like I was in pain.

"First thing she did was pull my pants down below my ass, then..."

I pulled my blanket over my lap and pretended like I was jerking off.

Toby giggled, Boden said, "You're such a fag."

I stood up and said, "What the fuck did I tell you about saying 'fag,' bitch? You know my cousins are fuckin' faggots! Only I can say that word!" Ever since a couple of my cousins and good friends told me they prefer eating cock I've been a bit more sensitive to the word "fag." I try not to say it, but sometimes it just feels right, so instead I tell others not to say it. It makes me feel better.

"You're such a fucking faggot hypocrite Donny!" he replied.

"I'm gonna fuckin' rape your little bitch ass one day, you might as well get it over with," I said, only half joking.

Toby giggled again.

"You're a fag," Boden said.

"Shut up and tell the fucking story," I said.

Boden continued, "so I'm face down, ass sticking out, and she's massaging my lower back and upper ass. Her hands came eerily close to my ass crack..."

"Oh my God I love that!" I exclaimed.
He continued, "so then she starts massaging my legs, and she spent most of the time on my inner thighs, and she worked really hard for a tip, because her fingers were like, grazing my nuts with each stroke up my inner thigh."

I tilted my head up and rolled my eyes back in my head, as if I was feeling her hands graze my nuts at that very moment. Boden continued, while Toby nodded his head in   agreement,

Boden said, "I got a raging boner under my towel and tried to fight it for a little while. Finally I said 'fuck it' and I just let it fly."

"I've seen your little Jew dick bro, the head barely makes it out of the foreskin when you get hard," I said. Toby giggled.

"Fuck you, you're a fag," Boden said, again.

"Look, if you want me to be a fag, I'll hold you down and pummel your asshole till you squeal like a pig. Is that what you want? You want me to be a big mapist?" I stood up and walked right in front of him, then looked down on him as he sat on the cot. I smiled like a creeper as I said, "ain't nobody's gonna save you boy." I loved threatening him.

Toby chuckled and said, "what's a mapist?"

"It's a man rapist," I said, "I don't rape chicks, that's disrespectful and degrading to women, I only rape little man- bitches like Boden." Toby Laughed out loud.

"Fuck both of you," Boden said, looking at both of us and pushing me away. I switched out of creeper mode and sat back down on my cot. Boden continued, "So I think she noticed that my dick was hard, and she started calling me her 'blonde angel'." He smiled at the thought of it. "Then she starts patting my ass, and then judo chopping my ass. She does this for a minute, then adds lyrics. As she judo chops my ass, she says 'masseuse' then as she pats my ass, she says 'girlfriend.' She repeated this like 10 times. It was really weird but kind of a turn on."

I was desperately waiting for the part where she jerked him off so that I had confirmation that they gave hand jobs.

"Ok, so what happened next?" I asked.

"Nothin' man. I was seriously considering asking for a hand job but there was a sign in my massage room that said 'DON'T SOLICIT SEXUAL ACTS,' or something like that, so I didn't risk it."

I was infuriated, "NO HAND JOB!? What the fuck kind of bullshit establishment is this? Yeah I saw that stupid ass bullshit sign too, but who the fuck actually takes it seriously?" I felt deflated and dejected.

"Well I'm sure they did give happy endings at one point, and some dumbass Marine probably tried to blow in the girls face or some shit, and ruined it for everyone."

"It only takes one to ruin the fun for everyone," I said gravely.

We all nodded in agreement and looked at the ground for a second.

"Well fuck, my appointment is in 30 minutes and all I can think about is getting jerked off by one of those Mongol bitches."

"Well, go ahead and be the Officer who gets court martialed for soliciting sex from an international worker." He pondered the thought for a moment, then smiled. "I would be so fuckin happy if you got sent home before your first firefight. Please do it."

"Don't tempt me, Boy."

"Why not? You won't do it, you're a pussy."

I stood up like I was gonna hit him. He held his hands up to protect his face and said, "get away from me bitch," I left him alone, sat back down, and started putting my uniform on, in a bad mood.

"Well fuck man, I purposely didn't beat off last night because I was saving it up to shoot a load on the Mongol. Now I'm gonna be so fucking horny I'm not gonna be able to relax during my massage."

"Well I say go for it Don," Boden said and quickly hurried away.

With Boden gone, Toby told me about his massage. He said that his masseuse brushed his nuts with every stroke. He told this to me with big, boyish eyes that made him look like a little kid who just saw a Ninja Turtle in real life. He was a real goody two-shoes, and would never in a million years have asked for a hand job.

I finished putting my uniform on, left the tent, and headed for the massage parlor feeling bitter.

The walk to the massage parlor was miserable. My dick was hard as a rock, and with all the blood in my dick, I couldn't think straight. Every fat, disgusting Air Force chick looked beautiful. The Mongol employees looked beautiful. When I looked down, even my right hand looked beautiful. I kept debating in my head if I would subtly ask for a hand job from my massage. I imagined the creative ways I could hint at a happy ending, all without being so blatant that I was reported and court martialed. I knew that my dick was going to be hard as a rock during the entire massage, and I was probably going to be dripping on myself.

I would spend the entire massage sweating in anticipation of asking for a hand job; I wouldn't relax, and I would focus on either trying to hide my hard on, or trying to maneuver it into the masseuse's hand as it grazed by my crotch region. I reminded myself of how incredibly stupid I can be when I'm horny, and remembered that every single time I have ever gotten into trouble--and there were many times--it was because I was drunk or horny. I second-guessed my decision to go into that massage with a loaded gun.

Two seconds later, when a hideous, crusty, old, wrinkled, female Army Sergeant First Class walked by- and I imagined my dick in her nasty, diseased, tobacco-filled mouth- I realized I had a serious mental problem and needed to fix it immediately to avoid court martial.

It was time to beat off.

I noticed a lone blue porta-potty on the side of the main street in Manas. It was oddly placed, almost weird looking, on a very busy street with hundreds of people walking by it every minute. Lacking more time to find a nice, clean, private, heated bathroom, I decided to stop in the porta potty for a quick beat.

Once inside, I took my right glove off, squirted some hand sanitizer on my right hand, then spat on it, and went to town on myself. It was about 15 degrees, so it turned out to be the coldest beat I've ever thrown. My hand became numb very quickly, and I realized that I had to be at the massage in 10 minutes.

I closed my eyes and focused, imagining that I was making vicious and powerful love to my ex-girlfriend doggy style. In my fantasy I slid my hand up her back to the back of her neck, carefully grabbed a handful of hair, and then tugged it back as I growled in her ear, like I always did. She turned around and said with a hood rat accent, "I ain't even tryin to fuck with dese niggaz. Nu uh. Ain't hatnin', dey can do dat boooo shit dey DAMN selves."

What the fuck? I thought, as I opened my eyes and pulled out of my dream. Someone outside ruined my fantasy. I stood on my tiptoes to look out of the plastic grate on top of the porta potty. There was a group of black Air Force chicks walking by, complaining so loud the whole base could hear. The one complaining was smoking hot and had a great body to compliment her poor attitude. I was annoyed, but I got right back in the fight and resumed beating the shit out of my dick, imagining plowing the attitude out of the obnoxious Air Force chick until she said the safe word.

With a strong work ethic, focus, and teeth gritting

determination, I was done in about five minutes. Not my quickest, but, given the circumstances and distractions, not bad at all. With my load blown life was completely different. The thought of nasty Eastern block-Mongol masseuses grossed me out, and I immediately relaxed. I was no longer concerned with whether or not I got a hand job. All I wanted was a nice, therapeutic massage to relieve the terrible knots I had in my upper left back.

I walked the rest of the way to the parlor with a huge smile on my face, and maintained that same smile when I opened the door. I made eye contact with the girl at the front desk, and held it as I approached her. My smile and energy were so handsome and charming, that again, I smelled her crotch as she yearned for me with a huge smile on her Mongol face. I returned her a sad smile, with one eyebrow raised, and shook my head as if to say "sorry, you cannot have this." She understood. As I sat in the waiting room around other Marines, I saw how anxious they looked. I felt bad for them. I knew exactly what they were thinking and how they were feeling. As an Officer always looking to teach something to junior Marines, I wanted to educate them on the importance of jerking off before massages that don't offer happy endings. Unfortunately, I was called by my masseuse before I got the chance to mentor them.

My masseuse was not the slightest bit attractive, although it's hard to say for sure. Every guy knows, that for 10 minutes after jerking off, nothing in the world is attractive. All sexual objectivity normally assumed by women is gone, and they are reduced to being actual people; with feelings, hopes, dreams, and even families who love them.

So who knows, my masseuse could have been hot, I just wasn't in a position to judge.

My masseuse directed me to remove my clothes and lay face down on the table. It dawned on me that I hadn't showered in five days.

When she stepped out of the room, I took my blouse off and smelled my pits. It was atrocious.
I took my boots off and was punched in the nose by the smell of my feet. It was like eggs and vinegar that had been cooking in the sun.
I took off my pants and was assaulted by the smell of my crotch. It was like shit, sweat, and balls stuffed into a horses hoof, and then kicked into my face.

I grew terribly insecure about my smell. For one, because I was still within the 10-minute window that allowed for concern of the poor girl's feelings, and more specifically, her olfactory glands.
For two, I became terribly insecure about what she would think of me. I'm not quite sure why I was concerned with my reputation amongst Russian-Mongol masseuses in Kyrgyzstan, but at that moment, I was very concerned that the 'tall, handsome, and confident Marine officer,' who was clearly full of himself, was going to be labeled a "disgusting piece of shit" by Eastern Bloc masseuses.

I frantically searched every drawer in the room for something that could make my orifices and glands smell less like death. I was hoping there was a can of air freshener I could empty into my asshole, but I couldn't find one. Alas, I found a bottle of baby oil that I thought would neutralize the smell of shit, so I bent over and poured it into the crack of my ass, hoping that it would have a positive effect. It dripped down my ass crack, into my asshole, then continued dripping down the back of my legs down to my feet. Gravity's a bitch.

Then I poured the oil on my feet, assuming oil always went well with vinegar, and put my socks back on, hoping to protect my masseuse from the stench of my feet. This proved to be a poor decision.

I sat down on the table and took a big whiff of myself. I still smelled shit and balls. I went back to the drawers and dug deeper. I found a small bottle that had a faint, faded drawing of a tiger on it; I screwed off the lid and took a whiff. It smelled amazing and powerful. I assumed it was some kind of lotion, like a Vaseline or mentholatum, and knew it would be better than nothing. I took a big glob of it and wiped it on my chode, then, without hesitation, grabbed a bigger glob and wiped it on my asshole. I closed my ass cheeks, hoping to spread it around and neutralize more death... and then, all of a sudden goosebumps came over my entire body, my mouth started salivating, my eyes teared up, and my asshole felt like someone was shooting a blowtorch into it. It was the worst pain I had ever experienced in my entire life.

The burning sensation in my ass was so bad that I thought I was going to vomit. The fire raging on the skin of my ass scared all the shit away from my asshole and back up my intestines, into my stomach, up my trachea, and into the back of my throat. I gagged several times, and threw up a little in my mouth. I was wincing like a baby, with tears dripping down my face. I had both hands on my ass cheeks with my sphincter and my cheeks clenched as tight as I could. I was hopping around on my tiptoes with my underwear around my ankles, and my mouth wide open on the verge of screaming at the top of my lungs. I was so angry I wanted to rip down every sheet hanging in the massage parlor and beat the shit out of everyone in sight, yell like a lion, and then defecate on everyone's faces; in a Tiger Balm-induced rage.

At 28 years old, I didn't know what Tiger Balm was, until later when I got back to the barracks and told my buddies the story. To which they responded "OH MY GOD THAT WAS FUCKING TIGER BALM YOU IDIOT!"
Yeah, thanks guys.
Anyways, back to the devils flame.

I hopped around looking for something to use to remove the substance that was causing my asshole and chode to rage on fire. I heard my masseuse outside say with a thick Russian accent, "Mister, are you ready for me?"

"NO, NO, NO, DON'T COME IN. Not ready yet, one second please."

"Okay, I come back."

I looked down and realized that my sock was the best option I had to put the fire out. I ripped off my right sock and rubbed it in my ass with long, hard swiping motions. I winced and my entire body shook as I wiped. I was still in terrible pain, so in a rage I ripped the sock apart and gave myself some more surface area with which to wipe. The pain began to subside, but still lingered bad enough to make me whimper. When I was out of sock to wipe my ass with, and the pain subsided to a more tolerable level, I leaned against the wall, sweating and out of breath, and pondered how I had the potential to be such a fucking loser. I was literally in shock that I could be so stupid. I should have known from the harsh smell of the substance that it might have had an adverse effect, like, the fires of hell. Hindsight is 20/20.

I looked down at my naked body, with shitty baby oil dripping down my sweaty legs, with one sock on my left foot, one half a sock filled with Tiger Balm and shit in my right hand, smelling like a chemical-rich, diaper creation lab; and then I saw my blouse on the floor, with the proud "US MARINES" name tape, my name "O'MALLEY," and my shiny silver bar indicating: MARINE OFFICER; and I started laughing hysterically. I shut my eyes as I laughed loud and hard, flexing every muscle in my body with the same intensity that I had when the fire was raging. I fell to the ground on my hands and knees and continued laughing. Finally, my masseuse opened the curtain and peeked in. She saw me butt naked, on all fours, in all my glory, bright red in the face, with my head tilted back, laughing without a care in the world. She said "WHOA," and quickly shut the curtain door.

Unfazed by the intrusion, I continued laughing uncontrollably for several more minutes, and eventually laid down on the table with my boxers on, and continued laughing until my stomach hurt. Then I finally gave her permission to enter.

"I'm ready," I yelled, still laughing.

She walked into the room and smiled confidently, not

the slightest bit embarrassed to have seen me naked, which was unexpected. I thought she'd be a little shy about it, but she was older, and definitely more experienced. Before she started she said in her Russian accent, "Why you have on one sock?"

"Oh, my feet get cold," I said, not knowing what else to say.

"Then where is other sock?"

"Oh, I ripped it." I glanced over to my pile of clothes; half of the Tiger-Balm-shit-sock was sticking out from underneath my pants. I smiled, then nodded to my left foot, "You can take this one off," I said, not wanting to explain further.
She took the sock off and said in her Russian accent, "Ooooo wow. What do you shower with boy?"
I couldn't help but laugh as I said, "Oh, the military soap they give us is no good."

"Oh, wow," she exclaimed, amazed that military soap smelled like eggs, oil, and vinegar, as she warmed up my muscles with her hands.
I told her that the biggest problem I had was in my upper left back, around the scapula, and that I wanted her to focus there. It was an old injury from my first deployment.

This is where my experience should have taken a turn for the better, since it's hard to be a bigger loser than I had already proven myself to be. But it didn't. In fact, I continued coasting down the road to shame.

She did a decent job warming me up and getting to the scapula. As soon as she put pressure on my scapula, I grunted under the pain and pressure of her hands.

"You are very tight here. I must work here for long time."

"Yes, please, you can spend the whole session on this part of my back."

She continued rubbing all around my scapula, and began using her elbow at my request for more pressure. She put the full weight of her body into her elbow, creating so much pressure that it pushed the air out of my lungs. Each time her elbow slid past my scapula and into my trapezius, I grunted loudly. The knots and scars around my left scapula throbbed on a daily basis, and were very sensitive to the touch. Her elbow, pressing down underneath all her body weight, felt like a jackhammer in my back. My grunt was a combination of the sound, "AHHH," with my teeth gritted, and the air being pushed out of my lungs by the pressure. Because she moved slowly, the first motion from lower back to neck worked out to roughly one grunt every 12 seconds. Then she started in the mid-back and worked her way up. One grunt every eight seconds. Then she focused on the scapula and brought me to one grunt every three seconds.

At this point there was a lot of noise coming from my room. To the untrained ear, it could have been assumed that a man was trying to get a nut off. Not surprisingly, three other masseuses pulled back the curtain and peeked inside to see what all the noise was about. Then I heard someone in another room, definitely an Air Force nerd, say, "what the hell is that noise all about?"

I began to get a little insecure about my grunting and tried to hold it in. By holding it in, I turned my manly grunt into a pathetic little whimper. She continued her massage and started laughing at me.

"Why are you cry boy? You look like big strong man. And you are cry?"

She kept laughing. I don't know why, but it really rubbed me wrong way... no pun intended. She kept laughing and repeating, "Why are you cry boy?" As if she found it immensely humorous that a big, badass Marine could be such a pussy.

I had a quick vision of choking her with my Tiger-Balm-shit-hand until she started crying, then saying, "Why are you cry girl? Why are you cry?"
The vision went away as quickly as it came.

I finally responded to her and said, "I'm not crying, my throat is clogged. AHEM." I cleared my throat.

She said, "Ohhhhhh okay" like a smartass. She kept laughing at the whimpers that I tried to turn back into grunts.

She whispered in my ear, "Don't cry boy, it's okay, you don't   cry."
I realized at that moment that I was probably the biggest, worst smelling, most disgusting pussy that she had   ever   massaged.

I was anxious for her to finish and get her filthy Mongol hands off me, but before she was done she had me lay on my back while she pretended to be a fucking chiropractor. She tugged and twisted my head and tried to crack my neck, whipping it from one side to the other, carefully, but aggressively, as brand new, bottom-of-the-class-chiropractors do. I couldn't relax enough to let her do it, so I flexed and fought her at every turn.

"Relax boy, relax."

I finally began laughing at the hilarity of some dumb Eastern Bloc masseuse attempting a Chiropractor's most dangerous technique, as I resisted her every movement. She probably looked like she was trying to twist my head off.

As I laughed I said, "I can't, I can't, I can't relax, just stop. Stop." At the end of that sentence my tone changed to *annoyed.*
She finally stopped and rolled her eyes, reinforcing that I was the biggest pussy she ever massaged.
She walked towards the curtains, and without looking at me she said, "You put on clothes, see you at front desk."

The few minutes that I spent putting my clothes back on were miserable. All of the humor had left my body. All that was left was shame. I felt immense, powerful, unadulterated shame about the events from the last hour. I looked down at my uniform on the floor and thought, *Marine officer huh? Yeah, sure you are buddy.*
My back was sticky from the oil that the masseuse used, and while it might have looked clean, it felt disgusting, because I thought about all the other buttholes that her

filthy hands rubbed against before she started rubbing my back. I wondered if she even washed her hands.

I put my skivvy shirt and blouse on first, then my pants, and finally my one remaining sock. I looked at the two halves of my Tiger-Balm-shit-sock on the floor. I would have normally chuckled, picked up the socks and stuffed them in my pocket, but instead I thought, "Fuck this bitch," and left the socks right where they were. I was already feeling so embarrassed that I didn't care if I lost even more of her respect by leaving my two half socks on the floor. In fact, I hoped the Mongol would walk back in, pick them up, and give them a good sniff.

I would like to reiterate; I was a Marine officer.
I walked to the front desk with only one sock on my left foot, shitty baby oil all over my body, the remnants of a small fire in my asshole, and no pride left in my heart. Once at the front desk, I gave the front desk girl a partial smile. She returned me a sad smile, with one eyebrow raised, and shook her head as if to say "sorry, you cannot have this." I understood.

As if I had not been shamed enough, I saw my masseuse talking with some of the other girls down the hallway. It looked like she was telling them a story; she held her hands to her nose, she held her elbow up, and she made a crybaby face. She was clearly telling the story of what it was like massaging me. The three masseuses listening were laughing hysterically.

Feeling like a complete loser, I walked out of the massage parlor and into the freezing cold, causing my dick to complete the transformation and shrivel up into an actual pussy. I hadn't walked two steps before I passed a group of my Marines. They propped up, smiled, and said with a crisp salute, "Good morning, Sir." I stood up proudly and returned the salute with a fake confident smile and a motivational, "Ooorah, Marines."

Once they walked past me, I let my smile fade, let the air out of my lungs, hung my head in shame, and headed back to the barracks feeling like I had let down the Marine Corps, and my country.

If they only knew…

MORE PREFACE

Hi, my name is Donny O'Malley, and after that story, you know damn well I'm not going to feed you the typical bullshit you read about war. This is partly because I had a fortunate experience with minimal casualty and tragedy, and partly because I want to be different. That first story is included purely because it's a good introduction to my childish humor, the rest of the stories are about the humor and frustration (much of it being sexual frustration) surrounding the last combat operation of my deployment.

Before you read further I want to make it clear that my combat experience in Afghanistan was weak compared to what many other Marines have done in the past, and even to the Marines who fought in the city to the south of me while I was there, in Sangin.

As exciting as some of my stories might seem to those who have never been to combat, they are nothing in the grand scheme of Marine battles and combat experiences. I am humbled every day by those who have gone into battle before me, into places much more violent and dangerous than the places I've been. I worship those Marines, and the battlefields those Marines fought on; Sangin, Garmshir, Marjah, the Korengal Valley, Fallujah, Ramadi, Baghdad, Hue City, the Arizona Territory in Vietnam, Korea, the Pusan Perimeter, Guadalcanal, Peliieu, Iwo Jima, Okinawa, Belleau Wood, Germany, France, and the list goes on.

I wish with all my heart I could have been there with those Marines, on all of those battlefields, to endure the misery and relish the camaraderie that shines in the worst of circumstances with a joke and a smile.

Instead, I was placed into a somewhat dangerous area, with a decent amount of IEDs and enemy fighters, but with much better training than those who had gone before me.

A lot of Marines died learning lessons the hard way in Afghanistan, making it easier for my unit.

I write about my experiences because I can, because it doesn't hurt me to do so. Those who had it worse than me, who saw more Marines die and get hurt, who patrolled through more mine fields, and who were not fully prepared for what they saw, don't want to write about their stories because it hurts to think about them. For some guys, the hurt is so bad that they can't live with it, so they blow their own fucking brains out or wash down a full bottle of oxycotnin (from the VA) with a fifth of jack. Oh, they also hang themselves.

I acknowledge this, and as you read about my experiences, and the horribly inappropriate, irreverent way in which I speak about them, I ask that you do too.

When I was in Afghanistan, the rules of engagement were fucking retarded. I mean that literally; only retards and officers/lawyers/politicians who sit in air-conditioned offices far from battle, could possibly come up with our rules of engagement. Every man who has ever left the wire knows my frustration with the rules of engagement.

ACTUAL JOURNAL ENTRY,

0900, JUNE 30, 2012
Platoon Cmdr/Platoon Sergeant tent, FOB Shirgazi, Musa Quala District, Helmand Province, Afghanistan

I feel like I'm going crazy in preparation for this next op. All I can think about is Marines hesitating to pull the fucking trigger. Everyone is so fucking afraid of shooting a civilian that they watch Taliban spot them from right-in-fucking-front of them, and don't shoot them. Because it COULD be a civilian. Well let me tell you this:

When you are dropped into an area that is 100% controlled by the Taliban,

When you know you are surrounded by Taliban because the ICOM chatter says that "the mujahedeen must kill the invaders and make sure they never come here again,"

When you see all civilians leave the area,

When you see middle aged males peeking around walls, hiding in trees, looking at you with binoculars, carrying bags big enough to fit guns, laying down in fields looking at you, laying down on rooftops looking at you, all while the ICOM traffic says "I can see the American tanks moving. I can see the patrol moving,"

When you see murder holes in all the walls,

When you know that the last four units to come to this exact same area have been attacked by the Taliban as they were doing ALL of these exact same things,
And after all this, we still don't have enough justification to shoot someone who looks like they are spotting us...

That's when you know some officers up high are very, very fucking confused.

This is fucking retarded. It's not an opinion, it is fact. When you throw a Marine rifle company into a FUCKING HORNETS NEST full of Taliban who are dying to kill us, you cannot tie our fucking hands behind our backs. We must have the ability to decide, with our own judgment, when someone is spotting us with the ultimate intent of hurting us. This MUST be our decision; we should never have to wait to be shot at first. EVER. That is asinine.

If Mothers of America is so concerned about our young men getting hurt, then they should throw a fit about THIS. They should be outraged that when Marines are thrown into the situation that I described above, they have to *wait to be shot at first* before they can shoot.

There is only one way to come back alive from this next op. And it is to come in FUCKING SHOOTING. No hesitation, no fear of judicial repercussions, only a fear of not pulling the trigger quick enough. We must make a statement as soon as the birds hit the deck that this group of Marines wants blood. That we crave to kill as many of them as we can in as little time as possible.

We must make them afraid to peek around the corners, afraid to hold up binos, afraid to carry ICOMS, and afraid to plan against us, because if we so much as THINK they're bad, were gonna fuckin' kill them. I'm convinced that this is the only way to stay alive out there. I'd be willing to bet a lot of young Marines agree with me, and a lot of Officers, who are worried about their careers, disagree with me.

I have a feeling this next op is going to be a lot more intense than anything we have ever seen.

Lance Corporal Artem Lazukin

Job:
0311 Rifleman

Unit:
1st Battalion, 5th Marines

Battlefields Fought On:
Sangin

Insert: July 5, 1989
Extract: March 29, 2015

Method of Extract: Self-inflicted GSW to the head

Text these exact words to a friend you haven't spoken to in a while,

"Sup bro, I miss your fingers in my ass."

"HEY LIEUTENANT! … Are you two holding each other's fucking hands?"

Unbeknownst to the world, Infantry Marines are actually the most openly gay-straight men on the planet; this story is just a small taste of the "gayness" that goes on among Marines.

GAY CHICKEN

1300, July 3, 2012
Smoke Pit, Musa Quala District Center, Helmand Province, Afghanistan

In July of 2012, Fox Company 2/5 was given one last chance to kill Taliban in Afghanistan. With the war winding down, and an organized troop withdrawal slowly beginning, we were trying to do less fighting and convince the Afghan Army to take over security for their own country. There were two glaring problems with this idea:

1. The Afghan National Army blows.
2. No one in Afghanistan gives a fuck about Afghanistan, but especially *not* the Afghan Army.

Battalion leadership decided to insert Fox Company into the heart of Taliban-controlled territory by helicopter for four days, to make things safer for the good Afghan people--one dead Taliban at a time.

This last nighttime helicopter insertion into Zamindawar was to "disrupt enemy operations." This was just a politically correct way of saying, "The war's over boys; go get your kills while you still can! Oh, and while you're there, help us Senior Officers get a few more Bronze Stars."

Zamindawar had become our favorite place in Afghanistan, because it was crawling with Taliban who were willing to fight. The area was controlled by the Taliban government; they had jails, hospitals, schools and a courthouse--and the Taliban had never actually lost control of the area. The largest disruption of Taliban operations occurred when a few other companies from my battalion went in there a month prior and had small battles with tanks, Cobras, jets, and artillery.

For reference, you can watch the entire experience on *National Geographic's Battlefield Afghanistan*.

After the battle, the Marines left the area, and nothing changed. After this last operation, we would be completely done with combat operations, and would focus on retrograde for our last few weeks in Afghanistan. Retrograde really meant weightlifting, eating, and some more weightlifting... with the occasional and annoying bit of work.

This was a huge bummer for us in the infantry. The most fun thing to do in Afghanistan was patrol, raid, ambush, and hunt the Taliban.

No hunting = no fun.

It should go without saying, Fox Company's last chance to score a few more kills before we went home was the most exciting time of our lives.

We had two weeks to prepare for this operation, and as usual my Company Commander (also referred to as the CO) did bare-minimum planning, gave a worthless Combat Operations Order to the Company leadership, and was annoyed if I asked him for more information.

We, the rest of the Company leadership, had come to expect this from him.

Usually, after our CO gave us a Combat Operations Order for an upcoming operation, we'd laugh at the stupidity and incompetence; we'd joke about how we were all going to die, and then the other three platoon commanders and I would get together to plan out the operation ourselves.

Once we formulated a decent plan, we'd walk into the CO's tent and brief him on the plan we came up with. He'd put his nose in the air, pause for a moment, and say, "Good, that's exactly what I wanted."

We'd say, "Thank you sir," with the utmost respect, then walk out and roll our eyes as we cursed his name.
The intelligence we received from battalion for this particular operation was worthless. The plan our CO made was half-assed, and all of us Lieutenants, Staff Sergeants, and even Sergeants, felt like our luck was running out. We had narrowly escaped death and

dismemberment on too many occasions already, and with this being our last mission, everyone was on edge.

The Marine Corps is full of stories about guys who were on their last patrol, or last mission, when they stepped on an IED and blew their legs off, and/or died. Naturally, we dealt with the fear by joking about it, but the words "last mission" were inherently nerve-racking.

The reason it was getting so dangerous (as if night time helicopter raids into Taliban territory weren't normally dangerous), was because the Taliban expected us, and knew exactly how we executed helicopter raids. They knew our execution because we had done sixteen of these raids as a battalion – all in a short period of time, and all in exactly the same way.

By this point in the deployment, the platoon commanders and platoon sergeants were disappointed that our battalion commander had not fired our company commander for gross incompetence. We realized that the reason the BC not fired him was because we, the Lieutenants, would always save our commander's ass by completely ignoring his plan and coming up with our own.
Then our company commander would take the plan WE made, brief it to the battalion commander, and he would look perfectly competent.

I was so fed up, that I convinced the other Lieutenants we needed to let him fail. We had to agree with his plan and let him believe it was great. That way, he would brief his plan to the battalion leadership, and they would all get to witness his tactical incompetence. It was the only way the battalion leadership would see what we dealt with during our entire deployment.

Just to illustrate the type of planning that my company commander did for a nighttime helicopter mission with over 100 Marines in a Taliban controlled area, I will describe his exact plan, in detail:

1. Land at night by helicopter, somewhere around ... here (points finger to map)
2. Enter a nearby compound, maybe ... here (points finger to map)
3. Decide where to go from there for the next four days (shrugs like it's 'no big deal')
4. Extract at night by helicopter somewhere ... further south (makes a circle motion with finger while pointing to map)
Ball game.

Someone give that man a Bronze Star with Valor; only Napoleon himself could have come up with a better plan.

Allow me to explain why his planning left my panties in a bunch:

While I make myself out to be a huge goofball, child, and irreverent idiot, the truth is the only thing I ever took seriously as an officer, and the only thing I ever fully dedicated myself to, was planning. I studied maps like our lives depended on it. I planned operations and patrols with more detail and scrutiny than I had planned anything in my life. Every time I went into a new area I felt like I had been there before simply because I looked at the maps for *that* fucking long. Almost everywhere I went in combat I had 20 possible scenarios planned out in my head with reactions to every one of them. And every time I came across an officer who didn't take planning seriously, I wanted to bash his fucking head in. Lack of planning = dead Marines = epic, fucking, fail. I'll be goddamned if someone died because I didn't fucking plan.

(Take a deep breath. Exhale. Woosahhhhh. Ok now don't take the rest of this story seriously.)

On July 3, all the platoon commanders and company commander for Fox Company drove to the Battalion Headquarters at the Musa Quala District Center to brief our CO's award-winning plan to the rest of the battalion.

These trips were always fun for me; they allowed me to visit all my friends who were stationed at the District Center, see some Wookies, and catch up on all the battalion gossip. Truth be told, almost every time I left the wire in Afghanistan was a fun field trip, but that's probably because I'm a child.

The District Center was right next to the Musa Quala wadi. It was the size of two football fields, surrounded by ten-foot-high walls of sand and sea wire, and had the tallest buildings in Musa Quala. The three buildings were roughly five stories high, and riddled with bullet holes and marks from explosions of RPGs and grenades. There was a helicopter landing pad, a chow hall tent, a medical tent, a gym tent and lots of berthing tents.

We pulled up to the District Center in a convoy of trucks,

which we in Fox Company called "Mobile Assault Platoon," led by my bestie, Sergeant Loya.

After putting my things in my new "room" (which was a dark, musty dungeon full of miserable Lieutenants and Captains working long and odd hours and never leaving the wire), I walked outside to the smoke pit to catch up with friends. I was shocked to see my old friend Johnny who was supposed to be at another base, 30 km away from the District Center.

He sat on a bench by himself smoking a cigarette, leaning back against a mud wall, with his legs crossed like a woman. His entire demeanor was very effeminate. He puffed on his cigarette methodically, tilting his head back and slowly exhaling, like a stuck-up movie star. Each drag from his cigarette looked like it was the most delicious and savory air he had ever tasted. He had strawberry blond hair, fair skin, blue eyes, and freckles-- he reminded me of Cate Blanchet. He had a skinny body, the confidence and swagger of a hippie who truly believes he is single-handedly saving the world, the energy of an ADHD kid, too much sarcasm, a permanently hard dick, and an inability to experience shame. In short, he was absolutely nothing like a typical Marine officer –making him fucking awesome.

I yelled at him from across the common area, not caring that there were a dozen other officers around.

"JOHNNY! What the FUCK are you doin' here?"

The large group of officers stared at me with judging

eyes, but as soon as they realized I didn't give a shit about them, they instantly didn't give a shit about me.

Johnny looked at me with a huge smile. He stood up and put his arms out as he yelled, "I came to see you, baby girl!"

I walked over with an equally large smile and extended my arms out to embrace him saying, "Gimme a fuckin' hug, right now."
He tilted his head down and narrowed his eyes into a creepy look, "Oh I'll give you more than a hug," he reached down and grabbed my dick. Not a poke or a touch; it was a very healthy grab.

I flinched and stepped back, laughing hysterically but slightly embarrassed because there were lots of other officers around. If they were all Lieutenants, I wouldn't have cared, but there were a few Captains and Majors in the crowd who I didn't know.

We hugged a long, lingering gay hug. I heard one of the other lieutenants scoff and say, "Oh great, they're probably gonna start making out now."

I didn't acknowledge the guy who said it. Instead I looked Johnny in the face and said, "Honestly bro, if all these fuckin' faggots weren't around I'd make out with you right now."

He nodded in their direction and said, "Fuck them, I'll kiss you right now." He paused to look me in the eyes, then he nodded at me and said, "You won't kiss me, pussy."

On cue, we both tilted our heads, closed our eyes, and went in like we were going to kiss, then backed out at the last second, like straight guys always do- and began giggling like little girls. I heard one of the other Lieutenants say with disgust, "Oh my God, are they serious?"

We continued to laugh as we caught up on the last few months of combat. He was the leader of an Embedded Training Team. His job was to live with an Afghan Army Company and teach them to not suck so fucking bad; it was a nearly impossible job. He had been getting into firefights with the Taliban in the Musa Quala wadi while patrolling with his Afghan Army Company. We joked about one radio transmission that me and the other Fox Company Lieutenants had been laughing about for the last few weeks.

Before I get into the story of his radio transmission, I should take a second to explain to the non-combat-leader-readers: whenever you're in a firefight, the commander above you wants to know everything that's going on, *as it's happening*. The trouble with their demand, is that when YOU are in a firefight, your number one concern is communicating with your subordinate Marines to understand where the enemy is. Your immediate concern is *usually* not communicating with higher command when bullets start flying at you. There are a few other things you might be thinking about in a firefight, things like:

Where are all my guys?
Is the enemy maneuvering on us?

What's the IED threat?

Can we maneuver?

Wait, are they sucking us into an ambush?

Do we need air support?

Where are my machine guns?

Did we bring mortars? No? Fuck.

Where are the stupid chicks in the patrol?

Are they pissing themselves yet or just subtly crying?

Does McCormick have his fucking head in the ground again? God dammit, he's goin' back to Headquarters.

Where are the prisoners?

Is Jackson using a prisoner for cover again? Fuck.

Why are those scumbags peeking at us from behind the wall?

Somebody shoot those mutherfuckers so they stop fuckin' lookin' at us.

Where is that machine gun fire coming from?

Are we shooting at a person, or a mud wall that a person *was* behind at *some* point?

God dammit, somebody tell me what the fuck we're shooting at!

These thoughts, among others, consume a Marine leader in a firefight. Needless to say it's a constant struggle to give your higher command the information they need, as quickly as they want it.

Back to Johnny's famous radio transmission.

While Johnny was in the middle of a firefight, the battalion operations officer, Major Tard, who I'm certain has Asperger Syndrome, (I could be wrong, I've been wrong before) asked for Johnny's situation over the radio. Johnny's call sign was HITMAN, battalion's call sign was WAR CROSS. This is what the radio traffic sounded like.

"HITMAN this is WARCROSS, what's your SIT?" (Situation)

No response.

Out in the wadi, one of the Afghan soldiers had a weapon jam. Johnny ran over to him under fire, showed him that his magazine was loaded in his AK-47 backwards, slapped the soldier in the back of the helmet as if to say "Come on bud! You're better than that" then ran back to his position, firing a few more rounds at a couple of shitheads who were shooting at them.

"HITMAN, this is WARCROSS, SITREP?" (Situation report)

No response.

Out in the wadi, Johnny saw two ANA soldiers holding their rifles over their heads, firing blindly. He ran over to them and used hand motions to communicate "Stand the fuck up and shoot like a man", and walked back to his position, shaking his head in disappointment.

"HITMAN, this is WARCROSS, need a SITREP!"

"WARCROSS, this is HITMAN. We're bangin' in the wadi, standby."

The sounds of automatic weapons and yelling filled the background of the radio transmission.

"Say again, HITMAN?" The Major had the same look on his face that he always had: pure confusion and despair.

"We're bangin' in the wadi! Catch you later."

This radio traffic says a lot about Johnny the man, as well as Johnny the combat Marine. He was as irreverent as they come. Needless to say, word of his radio transmission evoked lots of laughter amongst the Lieutenants and Sergeants in the battalion.

We caught up and laughed more, then finally I had to piss. I asked him to come with me so we could keep chatting, then shit got weird.

"Bro come with me to the pisser," I said.

"For sure," Johnny said.

"Wait, we have to hold hands," I said, initiating the game.

"I wouldn't have it any other way," he responded with that big creepy smile that made me giggle.

We grabbed hands and looked at each other like a gay couple who finally agreed to show affection in public. This was a game, taken very seriously by the both of us, called Gay Chicken. The first person to stop being gay – was gay, a pussy, and chicken.

We walked about twenty feet before someone yelled, "DON'T PUSS OUT, DONNY!"

I tightened my grip on Johnny's hand and smiled knowing that a group of Lieutenants twenty feet away knew exactly what we were doing. We walked another fifteen feet and noticed a large group of officers coming our way, about to pass us on our left. It was the Battalion commander and his posse. We both tensed our grips and moved closer to each other in an attempt to conceal our gripped hands. I really wanted to puss out and let go. Our Battalion commander was a self-absorbed Mormon fucking tool bag who was so disconnected from reality that he tried to convince enlisted Marines that drinking was pointless, and getting drunk was stupid. He was such a sheltered and naïve dork, and he would never understand that all the *cool* kids played gay chicken.

I heard someone yell, "DON'T LET GO!"

The Battalion commander was at the front of the posse, walking proudly, as if all the officers behind him were following him because he was such a great leader. To his left was a Captain, nodding and laughing at everything the BC said, as if his FITREP depended on it. Behind them were at least three Captains and two Lieutenants. We avoided the Battalion commander's eyes, and the attention of all the other officers as we walked right past them, but a few steps behind them was the badass Battalion Executive Officer (XO), Major Donelson.

Major Donelson had the respect of every single Marine in the battalion. He wasn't intimidating because he was big, strong, or an asshole; his intimidation was created by everyone's desire to make him proud. I knew he was a good dude, but I wasn't sure how he would feel about two of his front-line Lieutenants holding hands in public. I became very nervous and desperately wanted to let go of Johnny's hand – but my gay pride wouldn't let me.

I tried to look at the ground, but I allowed my eyes to wander too close to his face, and I was sucked into his gaze. He looked from my eyes, to the oddly close distance between Johnny and I.

He squinted as he attempted to register the situation. I squealed as I thought about whether or not he saw our hands. I had the same feeling I always got when I heard enemy machine gun fire off in the distance, and waited for a string of bullets to litter the patrol. My whole body was   tense.

We passed him by a few steps, and hoped we were in the clear. I held my breath. Then someone yelled, "HEY LIEUTENANTS!" I knew it was Major Donelson. My heart sank.

We both quickly let go of our grips and turned to face the Major.

"Good afternoon, sir," we said in unison.

He had his hands on his hips and his head cocked to one side, "Are you two holding each other's fucking hands?" He   looked   pissed.

I heard the group of Lieutenants laughing hysterically as they watched us from a distance.

At the same time, I said, "No, sir," and Johnny said, "Maybe,   sir."

My face turned red.

Major Donelson walked over to us. His demeanor changed from angry to curious as he looked at his watch and said, "Wow. We're what? Six months in? I would've expected this gay shit to start month three."

Johnny and I looked at each other confused, then looked back at the Major with smirks on our faces. The Major concluded the conversation, "Well, carry on boys, just don't let your Marines see. Although they're probably doing way gayer shit than that."

"Roger that, sir," we said in unison.

He walked away and we looked at each other in disbelief for a few seconds, then we lost it. We respected him for his understanding of what young Marines do. Even though we were Lieutenants, when we get together, we act like a bunch of Sergeants, who, when they get together, act like a bunch of Lance Corporals, who, when they get together, act like fifteen-year-old boys. All Marines of the same rank in a room together are like adolescent boys.

I said, "Bro, we have to declare a tie. There's no way we can call that."

"Agreed. We will live to play gay another day," he said.

Johnny and I spent a few more minutes hanging out, then wandered over to the group of Lieutenants who watched it all. We knew we were gonna have a slew of jokes thrown our way at some point, so we just faced the music.

One Lieutenant kicked off the comedy, "So now that Major Donelson knows you guys are faggots, are you gonna just be totally open or what?"

Johnny shrugged, "Yeah bro, I really don't see why not."

"I gotta tell my fuckin' dad first," I replied.

"Well, you're gonna' have to tell him you have AIDS too, cause' after that British slut he nailed at Camp Bastion, Johnny's definitely HIV positive," a Lieutenant said.

"No, no, that was HEP-C I popped for," Johnny replied. "The HIV is a non-issue right now bro. Don't be givin' me credit for diseases I don't have. It's not right. I have to earn it first."

"I heard that chick fucked a whole squad from 2/7," someone said.

"That is out-fucking-standing," I said seriously. "That right there is why we need chicks in the grunts. Talk about a force multiplier! I mean think about that squad's morale right now, they're all fuckin' kings!"

"Bro, that chick is in the wrong fuckin' business. I'm tellin' you, she needs to do porn," Johnny said, "I mean, she was talented, passionate, and had an exceptional work ethic. She practically put on a performance. And plus, she wanted me to plow her face just as hard as she wanted me to plow her pussy. Which was as hard as my skinny ass could plow, and she STILL kept telling me to go harder. I literally had to ask God for extra strength for that shit." Johnny took a puff of his cigarette. "He obliged." Everyone laughed.

"Fuck it bro, what's her name?" A lieutenant asked, "I need to experience this pussy first hand." Everyone laughed. "And by the sounds of it, I think I found my new ex-wife. I always wanted to divorce a porn star." Everyone laughed again.

"Shit I'm getting' kinda chubby right now thinking about it," I said bending over and readjusting my dick. "But you go get it homie, just make sure you wrap that shit and only pull your dick outta' your zipper. That way there's no skin-to-skin contact. You made it this far in Afghanistan bro, you wouldn't want a slutty British nurse to loosen up your last tourniquet."

"Word," he said, nodding and puffing his cigarette.

All of us Marine Corps Officers and upstanding gentlemen nodded and agreed about nothing.

I said bye to Johnny and moved on to visit another friend, a guy I was closer with than anyone at the District Center: Nick Garret.

Sergeant Jeremy Sears

Job:
0311 Rifleman

Unit:
2nd Battalion, 5th Marines

Battlefields Fought On:
Ramadi, Al Anbar Province, Iraq
Marjah, Helmand Province, Afghanistan

Insert: February 18, 1979
Extract: October 6, 2014

Method of Extract:
Self-inflicted GSW to the head

Text another bro, right now.

"I'm gonna fuck your face with the force of God. That chill?"

"I had never made passionate love to a woman's face before (I'd only fucked face), but I guess when you're in heaven, that happens."

All men are pigs; Marines are bigger pigs; Marine infantrymen, in combat, while hunting the enemy, are the biggest pigs. There is no way around this, it's always been this way, and always will. In between battles, warriors need to get this primitive if they want to continue maiming other human beings with smiles on their faces.

SCENT OF AN ANGEL

1800, July 3, 2012
Battalion Confirmation Room, Musa Quala District Center, Helmand Province, Afghanistan

Nick and I deployed together on the 31st MEU the year before. We slept 2 feet away from each other, worked out, danced, wrestled, argued, took turns beating off, and giggled like eight-year-old brothers throughout the entire deployment. He's a huge guy, 6 foot 4, and 225 pounds of muscle, with a chiseled face and blue eyes. He's so goddamn handsome it's annoying; he looks like he belongs on a Marine Corps recruiting poster. Nick played tight end for the Packers for a minute before he realized that he really didn't care about football as much as everyone else. So he quit, and a few months later he joined the Marine Corps.

Nick and I hugged it out and caught up on what we had missed during the last few months of combat. He talked me through the suicide attacks that happened just outside the base a month before: the Taliban tried killing the local Afghan Police Chief, Commander Koka, with a coordinated attack consisting of seven guys. One guy detonated his suicide vest too soon and missed the target, taking out one of his Taliban buddies. Talk about an air ball.

A few other shitheads followed after the blast with AKs, just in time for Commander Koka to pull out his pistol and blast them. When Koka ran out of ammo, another suicide bomber ran in and detonated close enough to put Koka in a coma, leaving him with brain damage that put him on the same reading level as our Battalion Operations Officer, Major Tard.

(I talk a lot of shit on the ANA and ANP, but Commander Koka was one of the most badass mutherfuckers in all of Afghanistan. He lived a front line warrior life, constantly under threat of death, and never afraid to get his hands dirty. Even Shitghanistan has rock stars; Koka was one of them.)

The rest of the Taliban attackers were shot by the Afghan Police who finally pulled their thumbs out of each other's asses and started defending their country. I actually watched some of this happen on the screens in the Command Center tent on my patrol base. All I could see were the suicide vest explosions and RPGs being shot at the medevac helicopters. It was pretty sweet.

We looked out Nick's window, and he showed me where everything went down. He told me which officers kept their shit together and behaved like Marines, and which officers behaved like despicable little bitches. He reenacted the way a couple of the pussies responded and we had a good laugh.

The way a Marine conducts himself under pressure will dictate his reputation for his entire career, so it's kind of important to not be a little bitch, ESPECIALLY an officer.

We laughed for a while, caught up on each other's lives, and I demanded he name his developing son after me. He declined, we laughed some more, and then I went to visit a few other buddies before the confirmation brief.

At 1800, I headed to the confirmation brief, where my Company Commander would show the Battalion Staff his tactical brilliance, and the Battalion Staff would show Fox Company how they were going to support us while we tried to step on the cockroaches in Zamindawar.

By the time I arrived at the confirmation room, I had been fucking around with old friends for several hours, so I was feeling very silly and very arrogant.

The confirmation room looked like the same scene that Hollywood has depicted a million times. A high ranking guy stands at the front of a room, next to a white screen with a PowerPoint presentation, briefing the plan for a mission; and all the lower ranking guys sit around listening. The only difference was that the man leading this brief, Major Tard, looked and acted like Charlie Chaplin, which made this scene much more comical than anything Hollywood has ever produced. This is no exaggeration, Google Charlie Chaplin right now, the pictures you see are of Major Tard, with a mustache, top hat, and fresh shave. The pictures are only missing the Marine Corps uniform.

Against my better judgment, I took a seat at the very back of the room behind a pillar. From behind my pillar, I had absolutely no view of anything. This was an intentional and childish act of both comedy, and defiance. I knew my buddies would laugh, and I knew that I was saying to every person in that room, "I don't give a fuck about anything that will be said here at this brief." I sat straight up with my notepad out, staring intently at the pillar that was two feet in front of me as if it was teaching me something important.

If I haven't already made it clear, I was a terrible officer.

Every Lieutenant I knew who walked in the room and saw me sitting behind the pillar began laughing. One Lieutenant said "Wow, Donny. Still fucking off. Love it."

I kept my act up as my Company Commander walked in. He looked at me and said, "Jesus, O'Malley do you have to make it that obvious?" He shook his head in disgust and continued walking to his seat at the table.

I acted confused, "I don't know what you're talking about sir." He just shook his head and ignored me. He knew I was being a jackass, and I think a part of him wanted to laugh, and part of him wanted to punch me in the face, but as my boss he couldn't do either. Plus, my childish behavior in front of all the other officers in the room reflected poorly on him as my Commander.

I placed my map on the bench next to me, intending to hold the seat for Nick. Some Major I didn't know walked up to the bench, picked up the map, and sat down beside me.

Officers get a bad reputation because some of them think that their rank gives them privileges that extend beyond their command, and this guy looked like one of those officers. He had a hard-ass look on his face, but I was indifferent to his rank and demeanor. By this point in the deployment, my body was so broken, I knew that if I survived and made it back home, I probably wasn't going to be a Marine much longer. This, combined with extreme arrogance and close proximity to death made me an even more terrible officer. So when this hard-ass-looking Major that I didn't know took my buddy's seat, I was thoroughly annoyed. I looked down at the spot that was just two seconds ago guarded by my map. I leaned towards him and looked him in the eyes as if he was another   Lieutenant.

"Hey, someone is sitting there, and the map in your hands was holding his place." I looked him right in his eyes and said it aggressively.

He looked confused and embarrassed and remorseful all at the same time. He probably never had a Lieutenant speak to him with that tone, and wasn't mentally prepared   to   chew   me   out.

"Oh, uhh, ok" He got up quickly and looked around, although he could have just moved down one seat.

"Can I have my map back?"

He handed me my map.

"Thank you, sir." I said the word "sir" like it was a dirty word. (enlisted guys know what I'm talking about.)

He squirreled away and found another seat.

Two seconds later I saw something that made my jaw drop so fast that it almost dislocated; something that made my eyes pop out of my sockets, and made my dick jump from 6 to 12. A blonde, blue eyed, civilian FEMALE sauntered into the confirmation room. She was, without a doubt, the most beautiful woman I had ever seen. Either that, or I was just painfully horny...I'd bet on the latter. I followed her with wide eyes and an open mouth. She sat on the left side of the room, giving me a perfect view of her luscious little body. I tried hard to avoid blatantly staring, so in the interest of being less creepy, I faced forward and peered out of the corner of my left eye. I felt my heart rate rise, my blood pressure go up, and I heard my dick yelling at me from under my pants, "YOU BETTER MAKE SOME FUCKIN MAGIC HAPPEN DONNY! I NEEEEEED THAT PUSSY!"

I waved him off and said, "shut the fuck up, dick!"

He said, "FU---" as I pressed my legs together and shut him up.

I realized that if I didn't get my shit together, I was going to be crippled by my primitive urge to inseminate the blonde in a porta potty. I used all the discipline in my body to put her out of mind and pretend like she didn't exist. It worked, for a short period of time. Fortunately, Nick walked in at that very second and took my attention away from her.

I got giddy and slapped my hand on the empty bench next to me and waved to him like I was a high school girl.

"Wow, nice seat bro. You got the best view in the house," Nick said as he sat down next to me.

"Yeah, aren't you jealous?"

"Kind of, actually."

"ATTENTION ON DECK," someone yelled.

We all stood up at attention as the battalion commander walked in.

"At ease Marines," the battalion commander said. We all sat down.

The brief began, and people began falling asleep almost instantly. I laughed to myself as I looked at all the faces around the room. Some looked serious, some looked annoyed, some looked skeptical, some looked confused, and some looked comatose.
I looked entertained. I looked like the hyper kid with ADHD in 5th grade who was always moving around and doing things to get attention.

The meeting was run by Major Tard, who, in the opinion of every single Marine in the battalion, was a belt-fed fucking retard. I don't say that as a joke, I used to nanny for an autistic boy in college, and I worked with disabled children after college, and I'm certain Major Tard had, at the bare minimum, Asperger's Syndrome. (I was wrong once in 2004, so I could be wrong here.)

The meeting went on.
These are the types of things that were discussed in the meeting.

"If one helicopter goes down, we will do this (Insert retarded plan here)."

"If you run out of water on day 2, we will do this_____."

"If the first wave of helicopters comes under fire during insert we will do this _____."

"If we lose comm with you at any point, we will do this _____."

And so on.

All important shit, but everything was done half-assed. They were doing minimal planning just to put a check in the box, without thinking about what it would ACTUALLY be like to be a grunt on the ground doing the things that they were talking about. The plan for a downed helicopter was especially stupid and made me angry. The plan stated that if a helicopter goes down, the Marines in that helicopter would be in charge of securing it against enemy forces while they waited for the TRAP team.

Everyone in the room knew it was stupid, everyone was thinking the same thing, and yet despite the knowledge that several helicopters went down each month, no one else said a word about it. The cowardice of every man in the room was beyond disappointing.

I scooted out from behind my pillar and waved my hand to get the Major's attention. He saw me and looked even more confused than he normally did as he said, "Uhhh, yes, Lieutenant?"

Everyone in the room was shocked when he called on me because officer's didn't usually ask questions during briefs, but if anyone asked a question, it certainly wasn't a Lieutenant. I could see the tension in my bosses face as he waited for me to say something obnoxious and make it seem like he couldn't control his Lieutenants. I politely asked a question about the plan that clearly indicated its mental retardation.

"Sir, if a helicopter goes down, it's very likely that all the Marines inside will be combat ineffective, so how could they be expected to pull their own security as they wait for the TRAP team?"

Major Tard's face turned red, he grew confused, and he responded the way he always did, "Uhhhhh, well, uhhhhh, the, uhhhhhh, we can't assume that uhhhh, all the Marines on board will be combat ineffective, so uhhhhh..." He continued shitting out of his mouth while nervously glancing around the room in desperate search of a way out. I actually worried for a second that he was going to lose his shit and start banging his head against the wall like the retard that he was. He sounded so stupid the battalion commander had to save him.

"Well, it sounds like we need to do some work on the downed helicopter plan," the BC said, "lets re-attack that tomorrow morning at the terrain model and move on for now." He leaned back in his chair confidently and motioned his hand to Major Tard, indicating he should carry on.
Brilliant Leadership.

As we sat there during the brief, I pretended to diligently take notes. What I was actually doing was writing the same thing that I wrote in my notepad during every combat order I had ever received since the beginning of my Marine Corps training. I wrote the words,

"PLEASE FUCK ME IN MY ASS IN THE PORTA POTTY" in big letters on the page of my notebook. I elbowed Nick and gave him a serious look, then used my pen to tap on the words to direct his attention to my notepad.

As soon as he registered my words he bit his bottom lip hard and stared at the ground, using all the strength and discipline he had as a Marine not to crack up laughing. Just seeing his response, combined with my love for my own jokes, forced me to do the same thing to prevent myself from laughing hysterically.

Nick must have seen me do that joke at least a dozen times in two years, but fell for it every time.

In need of someone else to fuck with, I leaned to my right and did the exact same thing to the Lieutenant next to me. I didn't know him well, and had never done it to him before, plus he wasn't a grunt like Nick and I. As soon as he registered the words he lost his shit and had to fake a coughing fit to disguise his laughter. I tried to look serious because most of the eyes in the room immediately turned in our direction.

"Are you ok bro?" I asked the Lieutenant.

"Yeah, yeah, I'm fine." He said.

The battalion commander took charge and made a quick decision. He said boldly,
"Drink some water Lieutenant."

"I will sir, thank you sir," the Lieutenant replied.
The BC wrote himself up for a Navy Achievement Medal with "V."
The brief continued.

When the Lieutenant was done coughing and sipping water he showed me his notebook. He had tally marks on his paper because he was keeping a tally of how many times Major Tard said the word "UHHHHHHHHHH" while briefing. He was at 46 times and he had been speaking for 6 minutes.

That's actually very impressive for someone with Asperger's.

Next came the news from Major Tard that woke us all up;

"Uhhhhh, well, uhhhhh, we have one slight situation that we are currently working on. Uhhhhh. The, uhhhhh, closest Shock Trauma Platoon at FOB (Forward Operating Base) Edinburgh is running low on all blood types except A-, and the medevac helicopters are in direct support of 1st Battalion 2nd Marines because they have a large clearing operation going on right now in the Kajaki District. But we are working on this to make sure that we support Fox Company with everything they need. But the mission WILL GO AS PLANNED."

Every single pair of eyebrows in that room was raised as high as they could go. Everyone in Fox Company, which was five officers and our aircraft controller, searched the room to make eye contact with each other. All of our eyes found at least one other pair of Fox Company eyes, and without saying a word, we all heard the same words in our heads, *Holy shit we are all REALLY going to die this time.*

Nick leaned over and whispered in my ear "Nice knowin'

ya buddy. I'll be sure to tell your family you died dishonorably."

I leaned in to his ear, "Thank you, they would have wanted it that way."

I turned to look forward, then I leaned back into his ear, "You know what, fuck it bro, I'm droppin' bombs on everything this time. If I'm gonna' die I'm goin' out with a lotta KIA's. Everybody's gettin' killed up in he-uh."

"Please take me with you," Nick whispered.

"Sorry bro, need you to stay back and watch the fort, besides you're much more valuable to the USA here."

"Fuck you."

"I'm sorry that was mean. I'll take pictures for you."
"Fuck your pictures," he said, leaning forward. I could tell he was hurt, he loved action and hated being behind the wire, just like I did at the beginning of my deployment. I felt   his   pain.

We went back to pretending to listen to the inspiring logistics brief, and then Napoleon stepped up to front of the room to brief Fox Company's entire operation. I expected my CO to add some fluff to make his plan seem a little more detailed than what he had already briefed to Fox Company, but to the shock of everyone in the room, he didn't. He stood up in front of a Lt. Colonel, 3 Majors, 10 Captains, and at least a dozen Lieutenants, and briefed the plan that would save Afghanistan, and win the war:

"Well sir, we're going to insert here, move to these compounds, assess the situation, and figure out what to do for 4 days, then extract somewhere around here."

He was done briefing his plan in record time, and the room went silent. Eyebrows raised, and eyes hit the floor in embarrassment. I considered a slow clap, I have no doubt someone would have joined me. I also considered letting a frag go and killing everyone in the room, thus improving the gene pool for future generations. Finally the battalion commander spoke, "Captain Anderson, do you have any, um, tactical control measures written out for your guys?"

That's another way of saying, "Have you ever been trained as an Infantry Officer?"

Captain Anderson said, "yes sir, I have some control measures, but I could always make more."

The battalion commander was as polite as possible, which I think is a pussy way to deal with an officer, "Yeah, um, I'd like to see some tactical control measures, some phase lines, um, casualty collection points, and some, some more detailed planning for your platoons. I think your boys deserve that."

My CO said, "Absolutely sir. I completely agree. I'll have that done right away."
I looked at Nick and said, "I'll follow that man to hell."

He laughed and said, "With him leading you, you're guaranteed to end up in hell, but not on purpose. Like I said, it was nice knowin' ya bro."

I just shook my head and tried to not think about my own death. I looked over at the blonde girl, and like magic, I was over the stupid, half-assed-retard brief, and finally felt like I had something to live for. I stopped fucking around, and got serious, REAL serious, because I could no longer ignore the only blonde woman in the Helmand   Province.

When she first entered the room, my initial thought was *what.....the.....fuck? Who? Why? How? How.......do I put my dick in her?*

Then I thought to myself, *Don't even fucking look at her Donny, it's not worth it, you're gonna get creepy and stare, and she's gonna catch you, and shit's gonna get weird. So don't even look in her direction.*

I took my own advice, and up to this point in the meeting, I did a pretty decent job ignoring her. I had no one to fuck with anymore, my jokes were old, and the only thing I could think about was inserting my deserving dick into this woman's warm hole, the hole that was meant for procreation.

To this day, I don't know anything about her, nor why she was there. I *think* she was a part of the District Stability Team, which is a civilian job held by a person with the purest heart; full of good intentions, and dead-set on risking their life while saving the world, one shit-hole at a time.

She looked to be in her mid-twenties, but most importantly, she appeared to be alive, fully conscious, and able to make complete sentences without assistance.

She had bright blonde hair that I desperately wanted to smell, big cold blue eyes, the most perfect skin I had ever seen; rosy cheeks, white teeth, and plump lips. Her body looked perfectly curved. Her boobs looked to be at least a full C, her butt had some jiggle to it, and I imagined she had just the right moves. She looked oddly young to me, as if she was in Afghanistan to receive elective credit for her "Sustainable Agriculture" minor.

Now when it comes to assessing a woman's looks, I have an incredible ability to see beauty in everyone- including the most unfortunate of God's creatures- so I'm usually not taken seriously by my friends when I say a woman is beautiful.

But because she was in Afghanistan; because I hadn't seen a woman without a veil in months; because I didn't know that blondes even existed in Afghanistan; because I had watched all the porns on my computer at least 1000 times; and because I was terribly, painfully, blisteringly horny; she was the most beautiful woman in the entire world.

Only a man who has been deployed could possibly understand what I felt for this woman at that moment. She was, quite simply, an angel.

I was so fascinated by the sight of her that it made me uncomfortable—it made my hands sweat. I felt like a child molester in the center of the ball pit at Chucky Cheese. I caught myself staring at her for minutes at a time. I stared at her and saw a vision of us twirling in a circle in the middle of a poppy field, madly in love. I had a vision of us making out somewhere on the FOB, possibly in the little tree line near the creek, by the food storage containers, at night, when no one else was around. I imagined her lips were the softest things on the planet. Her tongue was bubbly and sloppy.

Then, clear as day, like it had just happened, I saw my dick in her mouth. It looked like a perfect fit.

Never in my own experience, nor in any porn, nor between any couple, has a dick ever looked so beautiful in a woman's mouth, as mine did in hers, right there in that room, in my imagination. I closed my eyes and the vision became more real for me. I saw her look up at me with her big cold blue eyes; they were magical and I got lost in them for a minute. I imagined being on a spaceship in the galaxy of her retina, I kept making my spaceship do backflips. My dream zoomed out of her retina and we were magically transformed back into the poppy field. It was a beautiful day, with a light breeze, and a few clouds to make the sky even prettier. The poppies in this particular field grew higher than normal, providing us adequate cover for a midday blowjob. I looked all around me and took in my surroundings. I smiled. I was in heaven. I'm not religious, but at that moment, God existed, because only he could have created the heaven I was in.

All of a sudden I heard classical music. I looked down and she was smiling at me. She looked so happy to have my dick in her mouth. It was almost as if she had been craving it for the entire deployment, and now that she had it in her mouth, her soul was fulfilled more than God himself could have fulfilled it. I felt like fate had brought us together, I smiled at her; she started giggling/gagging as I petted her hair. Then the music got louder and started to sound familiar. I strained to hear it, then I figured out who was singing to me. It was Andrea Bocelli, and he was singing "Con Te Partiro" to me—to us. My dick went in and out of her mouth slowly, romantically, to the rhythm of Andrea's magnificent voice. I had never made passionate love to a woman's face before (I'd only fucked face), but I guess when you're in heaven, that happens. It looked like this, play the song and follow along;

(Slide in slowly) Co-ooooooon teeeeeeeeeee

(Slide out slowly) paaaaaartiròooooooooooooo

(Slide in slowly) paaaesiiiiiiiiiiiiiiii

(Slide out quick) che

(Slide in quick) non

(Slide out quick) ho

(Slide in slow and pet her hair) maiiiiiiiiiiiiii

Suddenly, the breeze picked up and blew a poppy plant into my left side. Then the plant leaned into my rib cage a little harder. I woke up from my daydream and realized that it wasn't a poppy plant, it was Nick, elbowing me in my side. I turned and looked at him with an angry look on my face. I was so annoyed I wanted to hit him. My dream was going wonderfully and I was royally pissed that he took me out of it before I busted my nut.

He leaned in to my ear and said,

"Dude you have no fucking idea what a creep you look like right now. I'm not kidding. If I was her I'd run out of this room right now and accuse you of sexual assault with your eyes. Really dude, come on. Have some respect man, that's not cool for her."

At that moment I should have felt shame. But I didn't, instead I felt sadness, because I wished my brother was there to see me. No one else on earth has caught me creeping more than my brother has, and coincidentally, no one else finds it more amusing when I get caught in creeper   mode   than   my   little   brother.

 At first I felt lonely missing my brother, then I became ashamed of my behavior, then, magically, thanks to my ADHD, both emotions were gone, and I focused back on the   angel.
I knew I had to stop staring, and I did, kind of. But I made a promise to myself that I was not going to leave the District Center without knowing how this angel's hair smelled.

Allow me to explain.
Since arriving in Afghanistan I went the first month without a shower. I slept in a tent filled with a powerful odor of sweat, balls, socks, and farts. I had patrolled through sopping wet, manure-laden poppy fields that were being irrigated as we walked through them. I had smelled rotting, burnt, and bleeding Afghan bodies, spent ammunition, homemade explosives, blown IED's, truck exhaust, dead animals, live animals and the

shitholes they lived in, a constant waft of human shit, a constant waft of human piss, and the piles of chicken shit I slept in because they were softer than the ground. The bottom line was seeing that girl's shiny blonde hair made something deep within in my soul ache to smell it.

I wasn't going ANYWHERE, until I smelled her hair.

The meeting finished and I spoke to no one. My demeanor was completely different. I was a man on a mission. I sat in my seat and watched everyone leave, but I focused on HER. She took forever because she was busy talking with senior officers about "Afghan Stability" or some other lame bullshit. I'd bet a paycheck that both those officers were thinking the same thing I was thinking. Fuckers.

Finally she began to walk out of the briefing room and I jumped out of my seat to get as close to her as possible. I was too late, there were two stinky Marine officers between me and her. I took a big breathe in the hopes I'd get a hint of something. I got nothing.

I thought for a second that I was a fool for assuming she smelled good. After all, we were in the boonies of Afghanistan.

My soul wouldn't let me hold on to that thought. Something inside me told me that her hair smelled magical. I stayed close behind her as I walked, then all of sudden she stopped and started talking to some fucking dork. I walked right past her and the dork, and took a deep breath through my nostrils, but I was too late. I got nothing.

I kept walking out the door, because anything else would have looked really weird. I stood outside and pondered whether or not I should go back for another olfactory resupply and risk looking like a complete dumbass...or if I should just go to the bathroom and beat off so I could think straight. I decided that it was absolutely worth looking like a dumbass for the chance to be in the same room with that girl and smell her hair. I gathered up my courage and walked back inside; she was facing me, so I couldn't be too creepy. I casually walked past her--not too close--and took a deep breath. I thought I got a tiny hint of something fruity. It gave me hope. It filled my heart with joy. I knew it was all worth it, but I wasn't satisfied.

I kept walking and turned the corner, headed back to the briefing room. With no better ideas, I leaned against the wall next to the briefing room, and pretended to read my notebook. I creepily peeked around the corner and saw her in the same spot talking to the same dork. I took two deep breaths in, then slowly began exhaling. I made my move and walked right towards her backside, my eyes focused intently on her hair. I thought I saw a halo around her head. The dork she was talking to could see everything I was doing, and I'm certain he became afraid of me, because when I'm on point, I'm just that fucking creepy.

Just when I got close enough, I slowed my step and took the biggest breath I have ever taken in my life. My nostrils filled with a thousand fruits, my heart sang "Hallelujah," my dick went from six to 12, and I instantly had a few images of shampoo commercials in my head. Pantene Pro-V, Head and Shoulders, and Herbal Essences. I saw a girl in the shower washing her hair and screaming "YES YES YES YES!" Then I saw myself slamming the blonde girl from behind in a porta potty with her screaming "YES YES YES YES!"

And with that thought, I didn't miss a single stride. I walked my happy ass straight to the porta potty and held my breath for as long as I could, with the image of her face and the smell of her fruity hair fresh in my mind. I squeezed my eyes closed and ignored the powerful burning stench of fresh hot shit; I ignored the fact that inside the porta potty was probably 130 degrees; and I ignored the sounds of dozens of people outside as I jerked my dick into a hot oblivion. I tried to go back to the poppy field image, but this time the poppy wasn't as tall, it was dry and dying, and the sun was burning my skin. I tried to hear the sounds of Andrea Bocelli singing my orgasm to completion, but he was singing off tune, and he kept forgetting the words. Finally I imagined her sitting on the porta potty begging me to cum on her face, and with that thought, I blew all over it.

When my orgasm subsided and I stopped grunting to myself, I came out of my dream and the image of her sitting on the porta potty with my cum all over her face disappeared and was replaced by the 600 detailed penises drawn on the back wall of the porty potty. Reality hit me really hard. I took in a waft of fresh, hot, shit. I looked down at the toilet and saw three feet of steaming human feces. I looked down at my dick. He was black and blue and he looked like he was crying. He looked up and me and said,

"What's your fucking problem dude? Don't you remember the fucking safe word? You're a fucking dick."

I tried to apologize but it was no use. Poor little guy. I choked his fucking brains out by mistake, and I'm not even into choking.

I looked down at my legs, I was sweating so much it looked like I was in the shower. I held my right hand up and looked at it with dismay. I was thoroughly disgusted with myself. I was disgusted with everything about me; my smell, my look, my thoughts the last few hours, my behavior, everything. Disgusted. I both repulsed and hated myself. I took a deep breath in preparation for a depressing sigh and the stench of fresh, hot, shit punched me in the nose and I almost vomited.
It was time to go.

I cleaned up with hand sanitizer, got dressed, slung my rifle back over my shoulder and exited the wooden porta potty. With one breath of relatively fresh air outside the porta potty, I felt better about my life. After I was 50 feet away from the porta potties, smelling significantly cleaner air by Afghan standards, I began to love myself again.

As I walked back to my room with my head down, avoiding all eye contact, and feeling a strong sense of shame, I was still hesitant to fall madly in love with myself again. But after hearing a group of Marines talk about how to fuck goats in a somewhat serious manner, I realized that there was no need to be ashamed. I was just being a Marine; and besides, I got to smell the scent of an angel.

Corporal Trey Jablonowski

Job:
0311 Rifleman

Unit:
1st Battalion, 3rd Marines

Battlefields Fought On:
Helmand Province, Afghanistan

Insert: June 8, 1990
Extract: May 11, 2014

Method of extract:
Hanging

Message an old battle buddy,

"I want you to cum inside me. Don't worry, I'm on plan
B, every day."

"I'm gonna get it Loya, I'm gonna fuckin' get it, even if it means my commission. With God and General Mattis as my witness, that pussy will be mine."

Two days before our last combat operation I heard the best news that I had heard since arriving in Afghanistan.

A reporter was coming with us on the op, but not just any reporter, a FEMALE reporter. The news brought joy and hope to my heart. I went from being consumed by maps, intelligence, and planning of the area we were going to raid, to formulating a plan to stick my dick in said-named-female. I had no idea what she looked like, but it didn't matter, she was rumored to have a warm vagina, and that was all I needed to sustain life.

I should probably keep stories like this to myself, but that would be selfish.

The Hunt Begins

0800, July 4, 2012
Platoon Cmdr/Platoon Sergeant tent, FOB Shirgazi, Musa Quala District, Helmand Province, Afghanistan

I was on my cot studying maps when my buddy Boden walked in and said with a huge smile,

"So did you hear O'Malley? The reporter coming to Zamindawar is a chick!"

"Get the fuck outta here!"

"Yep. Too bad she doesn't like fags." He pointed at me and laughed.

"Shut the fuck up nerd," I smirked condescendingly, "you can watch me plow her and see how a real man fucks pussy."

"You wish bitch, you don't have these moves." He did an impression of him fucking a girl. He held his arms out in front of him, pretending to grab imaginary hips, and then barely thrusted his hips forward and back with the same range of motion that a Chihuahua might have as it fucks. It was a pathetic reenactment of a gut beating, and I found it hysterical. I cracked up laughing.

"Ahhhhhhh hahahha. Are you fucking kidding me? Is that how you beat guts you little bitch? I had a pet rat that could fuck more aggressively than that! Lemme show you how to fuck pussy."

I walked towards him and pushed him out of my way, then I walked to his cot, threw one leg up on it, and proceeded to give him a lesson in how to beat guts like a man. My lesson was complete with visual demonstrations and step-by step audio instructions.
As I was giving my lesson, Sergeant Mendez walked into our tent, saw me, and stopped in his tracks. I looked him in the eyes and made a quick decision to continue my instruction. Had I stopped, I would have been judged as both an immature child and a pussy. However, by continuing my lesson with no shame, I showed him that although I was an officer, always looking to educate—I was also a raging pervert at heart, just like him, and every other enlisted Marine in the Marine Corps.

Sergeant Mendez had a great sense of humor, so he smiled and yelled, "yeah sir! Get it!"

He came over and gave me a high five.

"That's how it's fuckin' done, sir! You should come over to the Sergeant's tent sometime, we got some good wifey videos we watch and critique, and my cheating whore of an ex-wife was practically a porn star. As long as you don't mind my Mexican dick you'll really enjoy yourself"

"Well I'm always down to learn new things Sergeant, and I've got nothing against Mexican dick. Hell, I'm half Colombian myself, so I can appreciate a good Latin hog. Plus, I'm sure you boys have some good pointers for me."

"Oh no shit, sir, you got that Irish and Colombian sausage?" He held up a fist bump and we laughed, "but for real sir, I put on a good show," he winked.

Staff Sergeant Flores broke up the fun and said "Ok, excuse me gentlemen, I'd like to get back to being less gay."

I yelled, "FUCK YOU! You were humping your chair just a few minutes ago." He was such a phony.

His face was completely serious as he hid his shame, "I uhhh, I don't think so, sir." His eyes darted around the room, "I would never behave like that around other Marines, especially not around junior Marines."

He was so full of shit I yelled, "You lyin ass bitch!"

"Sir, I don't think it's appropriate to call a Staff NCO a liar. I'm gonna' go back to my desk and finish my show. If you need anything please knock." He was such a smartass, and I loved it.

The audience dissipated and I resumed attempting to learn about this reporter from Boden.

"So is she hot?" I asked.

"Don't know. Supposedly she gets in today."

"Hmmmm. What paper is she with?"

"I think the Union Tribune."

"WHAT! That's fuckin' bullshit! Golf Company gets National Geo-mutherfucking-Graphic and we get the San Diego Union Tribune?! What is wrong with this world! Don't they know the most charismatic Officer in this fucking battalion is in Fox Company?! FUCK THAT! They should be sending us NB-mutherfuckin-C, or even better, Anderson-fucking-Cooper!"

I drooped my shoulders in defeat and sat down on Boden's cot.

Boden tried stealing my thunder, as usual, "Yeah I know right, and I'm also the hottest Lieutenant in the battalion too, so they REALLY fucked up." He loved the sound of his own jokes.

"Ok, you might have a prettier face than me, bu-"

"I definitely have a much prettier, and less cratered face than you, Donny."

"Ok, touché, the adolescent acne bomb hit me pretty hard. But your body is fuckin' garbage. You got the body of a 12-year-old boy. Look at all this baby fat right here," I reached over and pinched his baby fat.

He slapped my hand away and said, "Don't touch me fag."

I stood over him and said, "Don't be jealous boy. If you follow my teachings you can be 210 pounds of pussy crushing, Taliban killing, 12 year old boy raping machine." I put him in a headlock and grabbed his ass as I whispered in his ear, "better watch that cute blonde ass tonight. You might end up my next victim." He struggled and I let him go. He pushed me away and said, "Dude, you seriously have issues."
I loved making him uncomfortable.

"Yeah, I do have ONE tiny issue," I said, "it's that I'm so horny I would seriously consider raping you." I shrugged, "at least I can admit my faults."

"Yeah, well if I had faults I'd admit them too."

I laughed, "That's my line asshole." He chuckled.
We both sat back down and resumed our duties as Marine officers and Gentlemen.

4 hours later...
1200, July 4, 2012
Platoon Cmdr/Platoon Sergeant tent, FOB Shirgazi, Musa Quala District, Helmand Province, Afghanistan

I woke up from a nap to the usual chatter of Marines coming in the tent and being productive while I was sleeping. Sergeant Loya, my section leader and close friend, came into the tent and sat on my cot. We had incredible respect for each other, powerfully gay love for each other, and we joked around constantly when we weren't being serious.

"What's goin' on, sir?"

"Oh, just getting some work done."

He looked me up and down, making light of the fact that I was still in bed.

"Yeah, I can see that, sir. Would you like a cup of coffee this morning? Can I get you anything?" He said it like a smartass.

"No, no, no, you're too kind, Sergeant Please, can I get YOU a cup of coffee?"

"Well now that you mention it, sir, that sounds great."
I got up, reached over to Staff Sergeant Flores' desk and grabbed the pot of coffee that he had already brewed for himself, and only himself. He didn't share his coffee very often. I poured a cup for Sergeant Loya with a big smile.
"Brewed this fresh just for you, devil dog."

We both laughed at the obnoxiousness of taking Staff Sergeant Flores' fresh coffee while he was gone. "Can I get you some creamer and sugar, Mr. Loya?"

"Oh that would be lovely," he said with a smile.

We were laughing like mischievous children when Staff Sergeant Flores walked in the tent. He looked right at Loya and I. He walked over to my desk, stopped and stared at the coffee pot for about five seconds, then said, "so who can tell me how my coffee pot ended up on your desk," he leaned forward and took a closer look at the amount of coffee in the pot, "with exactly one cup less coffee in it than it had before?"
He looked right at me like a smartass. Loya and I looked like kids who were caught stealing from the cookie jar.

I said with a serious face, "actually, Staff Sergeant, that's just the damndest thing I ever saw. Loya, do you know how this got here?"

"No sir, no idea, it was there when I got here."

I stood up and put my hand on Staff Sergeant Flores' shoulder, "well, hey there, Staff Sergeant, I'm gonna' go ahead and assume responsibility for this. This situation needs a fall guy, and I think I'm the guy."

"I don't want a fall guy, I want one more cup of fucking coffee in my coffee pot."

"Consider it done." I said with a smile.

"Thank you, sir." He said as he sat down at his desk and looked at me out of the corner of his eyes with an evil look. Five seconds later he busted up laughing. "I'm just kidding sir, take whatever you want, you're the only one in this tent who can have my coffee, but that's because I like you. Don't you forget that."

"Staff Sergeant, I want you to know that if I die, you can have all my stuff, and if I had a couple wives, you could have them too. And that's because I like you."

"Well I love my wife, but I'll take everything else, just don't forget to write all your computer passwords on a piece of paper," he said. We both laughed.

Loya and I resumed talking.

DONNY- "So, do you know about this reporter?"

LOYA- "Yeah, actually I just saw her in the CO's tent."

DONNY- "No fuckin way! How is she? Hot?"

LOYA- Loya shrugged, "Umm....She's alright."

DONNY- "You gotta give me more than that."

LOYA- "She's blonde, tall, skinny, cute."

DONNY- "Oh my God, That sounds amazing. What am I missing? Tits?"

LOYA- "Nothing noticeable."

DONNY- "Ass?"

LOYA- "Can't tell."

DONNY- "How's the face?"

LOYA- "Meh...it's cute."

DONNY- "Well that sounds drop dead gorgeous to me."
Loya cracked up.

LOYA- "Well don't get me wrong sir, I'd fuck her if I
wasn't married, but if I put my wife next to her its like
night and day."

DONNY- "Ok, ok, but your wife is really hot, so that's not
fair. I just need to see this chick and decide how much
trouble I'm willing to get in to nail her on base."
LOYA- "Well she's in the CO's tent right now, we could
stop in and just bullshit with First Sergeant and Gunny.
Maybe you could come up with something to ask the CO
and then weasel your way into a conversation with her."

DONNY- "Yeah, that's gonna' happen. Lead me."

LOYA- "Follow me, young Lieutenant."

DONNY- "Bitch I'm older than you!"

LOYA- "Eh, whatever, it's fun to say."

I got dressed and followed Loya to the CO's tent. Just as I
opened the door to the CO's tent, the reporter and her
cameraman walked out. I was literally blown back, as if
there was a huge gust of air that blew out of the tent as I
opened the door. I saw the most beautiful woman in the
entire world, literally. She made the blonde girl from the
District Center look like dirty laundry. I fumbled my

words so badly I don't remember exactly what I said, but it was something to the effect of, "Oh, hi, you're the reporter I keep hearing about, ummmm, hi."

She was nice, despite the fact that I sounded like a dumbass, and said, "Yes I am, I'm Martha, nice to meet you." Even her voice sounded beautiful.

"I'm Donny, and this is my hero, Sergeant Loya." I put my arm around Loya and smiled.

Loya smiled and said, "He's always trying to talk me up. I'm really not that cool, but it's nice to meet you." He shook her hand.

I shook the camera guy's hand and we all stood around uncomfortably for a few seconds. I was waiting for her to say, "Oh, you're the Fire Support Lieutenant, the one that everyone calls the 'Grim Reaper', it's such an honor to finally meet you, I'd love to interview you and make you the featured Lieutenant in my article on Fox Company, and then when we're done with the interview, I would love it if you stuck your dick in my sopping wet pussy and blew your load so deep inside me that a part of you stayed in me forever."
But she didn't.
Instead she said, "Well it was nice meeting you guys, we've got to get going, but I'm sure we'll talk again soon. Take care."
I played it cool and said good-bye, but deep down I felt like an angry, sore loser. Once they were gone, Loya looked at me and said, "Well that was a bust."

I stood there like a statue and watched her walk away until she was out of sight. I held my position, squinting angrily, looking like Clint Eastwood in the Wild West as he plans to kill someone.

"I'm gonna get it, Loya, I'm gonna fuckin get it, even if it means my commission. With God and General Mattis as my witness, that pussy will be mine."

"I like you're style, sir. You'll get it. I have faith."

Loya and I did what we always did. Lift weights and talk about killing.

Sergeant Jody Tetzlaff

Job:
0311 Rifleman and 0317 Scout Sniper

Unit:
3rd Battalion, 3rd Marines

Battlefields Fought On:
Fallujah, Al Anbar Province, Iraq
Helmand Province, Afghanistan

Insert: May 2, 1983
Extract: December 16, 2009

Method of Extract:
Self-inflicted GSW to the head

Text a bro right now,

"Are you feeling like a little whore today? Because I sure am ☺ "

Later that day I wrote a journal entry that expressed my powerful love for America.

My love for my Corps and country was, and still is, overwhelming. No woman except my Mom and Grandma will ever be loved as much as I loved my Marines.

ACTUAL JOURNAL ENTRY,

2100, JULY 4, 2012
Platoon Cmdr/Platoon Sergeant tent, FOB Shirgazi, Musa Quala District, Helmand Province, Afghanistan

I just flew the American flag on base and took a picture with my battle buddies. It was truly amazing. Just before we flew the flag the Lieutenants in my company served chow to the Marines on our FOB. It was a goddamn feast, with way more food than anyone could eat. Steak, ribs, turkey breasts, sausages, amazing. It was such a blast. We made fun of each other the entire time and provided entertainment for the Marines. It was like a comedy food show. The other guys kept yelling at me and saying I was FIRED for not serving the grapes and barbecue sauce fast enough. We started calling it "Hells Kitchen." I pretended to cry, telling them how much, "I need this job, it's all I have." Then, when I would politely offer Marines barbecue sauce, if they said "no thank you, sir," I would respond quickly "go fuck yourself then," or "fucking selfish pig," and they got a real kick out of it. It was a blast. I kept yelling "AMERICA!" as I slapped grapes and barbecue sauce on guys' plates. I can't even tell you how proud I am every single fucking day to be an American. Even more so, to be a U.S. Marine.

So this next Op is pretty fucking dangerous, even borderline stupid. This, coming from me, says a lot, because I love everything dangerous. The more dangerous the better, for *me*, but that is NOT the case for the young Marines. Not everyone is willing to die for the kind of pointless missions we are getting. A lot of guys are wondering what the purpose of our missions is. Some don't think it's worth losing Marines' legs and lives. Our mission is pretty much to take as many Taliban off the battlefield as we can before we leave this country. Since we are fucking Marines, and we love the idea of being told to kill anything, 90 percent of us are PUMPED to get dropped into the middle of a dangerous area and kill everything we can. But a few, including some leaders, don't think it's worth it.

Lucky for us, we don't have a choice. When we joined this beautiful Corps we agreed to kill whoever the fuck the US gov't told us to. So bottom line is, I'm pumped to go out there with our medium machine guns blazing, our mortars dropping, and Hellfires coming off Predators in the sky. I expect the compound I'm in to be riddled with machine gun fire while my team drops bombs. We'll be safe behind cover once we get into the compounds, but The Marines up on the roofs are the ones who are in danger. I hope we all make it home alive.

Semper Fucking Fi!

Corporal Farrell Gilliam

Job:
0311 Rifleman

Unit:
3rd Battalion, 5th Marines

Battlefields Fought On:
Sangin, Helmand Province, Afghanistan

Insert: September 29, 1988
Extract: January 9, 2014

Method of extract:
Self-inflicted GSW to the head

Text this to a bro,

"Dude, I don't know why, but I have a weird urge to fuck your face in backwards. That chill?"

"Fuck the fuckin' CO, when you need clearance to kill someone, you better fucking ask ME, and no one else... is that clear?"

Afghanistan frustrated me to the point that I had to take matters into my own hands. By taking matters into my own hands, I mean I disobeyed orders and came up with my own. Why? Simple- because to me, while I'm in Afghanistan, trying to make life better for Afghans who don't care, a U.S. Marine's life is worth more than a million Afghan lives. This is not opinion, this is fact.

MINDFUCK

2200, JULY 4, 2012
Burn Pit, FOB Shirgazi, Musa Quala District, Helmand Province, Afghanistan

Afghanistan can be a very frustrating place, especially when senior officers scare younger guys into thinking that they'll be punished for taking a bad shot and hitting a civilian. The nature of war is foggy and uncertain. Very often, civilians get hurt by both sides of the battle, and it is nothing less than tragic. We knew we were there to help the good people of Afghanistan, and help them build government infrastructure that was strong enough to win against the Taliban.

The problem with the end of the war in Afghanistan was that American military Officer's were getting their careers threatened by civilian casualties. It started from Hamid Karzai threatening our President with civil unrest if we didn't reduce civilian casualties. The President then told our General's that if they have too many civilian casualties, they'll be relieved. The Generals told the Colonels the same thing, and the Colonels told the Lt. Colonels, and they told their Captains, who told their Lieutenants, who told their junior Marines,

"Even if you see a middle aged male that is exhibiting ALL the signs of an insurgent with intent to kill you, you CANNOT SHOOT HIM until he shoots you first."

Except for me. This Lieutenant didn't drink the cool-aid, and didn't buy the bullshit.

Allow me to explain something about me.

Prior to deploying to Afghanistan, I read dozens of books on Afghanistan history, counter-insurgency, counter-intelligence, and guerilla insurgency. I make myself out to be completely irreverent, but, truth be told, I took our deployment more seriously than I have ever taken anything in my life. I did more studying, reading, questioning, training, and preparing than I ever will about anything for the rest of my life.

The training the Marine Corps gave me was incredible, and within that training was embedded a powerful message that I believed with all my heart:

The mission is to win the hearts and minds of the people; if we hurt the people, we lose the mission.

I believed in the mission and gave my heart and soul to the good people, until I noticed something incredible.

The people we were there to help, often times, didn't really give a fuck about our help. They would LIE, cheat and steal, and say anything to get whatever they could from us, and then go back to sympathizing with the Taliban. Their sense of loyalty to their country is non-existent, their ability to lie and bullshit is better than any scummy lawyer I've ever seen in a movie, and their willingness to flop sides is inspiring to Lebron James. I went to Afghanistan with pure intentions, but within one month in the Helmand province I knew with 100% certainty that we were wasting our time trying to make a better life for them. I can't speak for all of Afghanistan, I can only speak for Helmand, but I can say with confidence that they are so fucking primitive, incestual, and uncivilized it's just not possible for them to become anything more than a third world shithole. The water they drink is so filled with bacteria, and their desire to fuck little boys, fuck their cousins, and oppress their women is so innate, that they simply can't evolve as a species. I have hundreds of vivid memories of young, old, and middle aged men wiping their ass with their hands in public, chewing on their own feet like retards while sitting on the side of the street, getting 12-year-old chai boys ready for their daily ass pounding, and then eating their food with their hands. I really do wish I was exaggerating, but this is the truth about Afghanistan that not one single officer in the entire fucking world will tell you.

Except me. #SharingisCaring #ZeroFucks

My brain tried desperately to hold on to the mission, which was the **people**, but it was a hard fight, because holding on to that mission meant waiting to be shot at before we could shoot those we knew to be bad.

One part of my brain was telling me,

"Fuck these lying mutherfuckers, fuck these Afghan Army pieces of shit who won't fight for their own fucking country, and fuck my boss for telling me I have to wait to be shot at before I can protect my Marines, who I love like my little brothers. This is fucking war, and as a

Marine officer it's my job to kill pieces of shit and make sure that a bullet doesn't hit one of my 120 little brothers. If that means I kill this asshole who keeps peeking around a corner, then so be it. If I'm wrong, and he was just a nice guy being nosy, it's a tragedy of war; but I'll be god dammed if the biggest tragedy of this war is my little fucking brother."

The other side of my brain, the part that absorbed my training as a Marine said to me,
"No, no, no, the CO gave an order, and I have to follow it. Even though I know that guy is bad, I can't shoot him, and I cannot allow anyone to shoot him, until he shoots us first. That's the order."

My training taught me better, my research taught me better, and I KNEW the mission demanded better. But it didn't matter once I was walking through minefields and getting shot at. It didn't matter once I saw Marines get maimed, or coming inches away from getting maimed on hundreds of occasions in the midst of a population and enemy that knew we were eventually going to leave the country.

All that mattered were my little brothers coming home alive.

Marine Corps tradition demands that all orders are followed without question. When someone says "TAKE THAT HILL," Marines are expected to do it instantly, knowing damn well they'll probably be chewed up by a machine gun on the way to the top. This mentality is the only reason we were able to win all the large battles that we have won.

Unfortunately for us, this counter-insurgency war we're fighting makes our "take that hill mindset" very difficult to maintain. This war requires an unbelievable amount of thought and strategy. This war requires constant second-guessing. Everything must be thought out and questioned a dozen times, to the point that you're sick and tired of questioning, and just want to shoot and blow up everything.

This kind of war has traditionally been fought by Special Forces and the Army, but because Marines can do anything, we've been doing it, and doing it well. (Except for me)

I've had Korea and WWII vets say to me, "You guys have it harder than we did. We just killed everything, and had a blast doing it. But you guys with all your rules, and politics, I can't imagine having my hands tied like that. That's a mindfuck."

They're absolutely right. It's a mindfuck like no other. It's a mindfuck that alters the brain for life. A Marine who has had his mind FUCKED by counter insurgency combat has some deep-rooted demons inside. He's angry at the Taliban, the Afghan people, the Afghan gov't, and the US gov't for throwing him into a minefield and tying his hands behind his back.

It doesn't stop there. Some guys have been mindfucked further by the rocks that were thrown at them by Afghan kids. Some guys have been mindfucked by the kids they became friends, with who the Taliban killed for "sympathizing" with us. Some guys have been mindfucked by their interpreters, who they became very close with, who turned out to be feeding intel to the Taliban. Some guys were mindfucked by the kids they hurt by mistake during a gunfight. Some guys were mindfucked by the kids they saw step on a Taliban IED and blow to pieces. And of course, many guys had their minds fucked when they watched their buddies blow up while patrolling down an alley that they KNEW was a minefield, just so that an officer could tell his boss that his unit "has the area under control with a constant patrolling presence."

Everything is a mind fuck, and no one understands, except those who were there.

So how did I deal with this mindfuck while I was there?

I thought long and hard about what would fuck my mind the most out of everything I was experiencing in Afghanistan, and my answer was simple. If one of my guys died because we were hesitant to pull our triggers, I would have nightmares for life. If a guy dies in a gunfight or by a bomb, that's war; and when I joined the Marine Corps, I accepted the fact that guys, including me, were gonna die. But if a guy died because of something I, as an officer, had the power to prevent—if a guy died because of a cancerous and irresponsible "don't-shoot-until-they-shoot-us" mentality that permeated throughout the company—my mind would be fucked for life. I'd feel like a coward of a man, and I'd hate myself for not doing more.

So I disobeyed orders, I did what my conscience needed, and what I thought all my little brothers deserved. I went behind my boss' back, and a few at a time, I pulled in the guys who ran the company, the Sergeants. I made it very fucking clear that we will not wait to be fucking shot at before we kill those we know to be bad.

I gathered up four Sergeants near the burn pit the night before the operation and brought them into a huddle. I was angry as I spoke.

"Listen the fuck up. This fucking don't-shoot-till-they-shoot-us bullshit is gonna make me go insane and call a broken fuckin' arrow up in this bitch.

Fuck what the fuckin' CO said, he's tryin' to save his fuckin' career, and that bullshit has no place out in Taliban Country. You go back and tell your boys that, according to the rules of engagement, if they feel like they're in imminent danger, they can waste whoever the fuck is making them feel that way. If someone peeking around a corner is making your boy feel threatened, fuck em'. They'll learn quick not to peek around the fuckin' corners. Your Marines need to stop fucking hesitating, and stop asking for permission to shoot if they feel threatened. If it's a bad shot, this is fucking war, so it's too fucking bad. If for whatever reason, you're not sure about taking a shot, ask me. Fuck the CO, if you want clearance to kill someone, you better fucking ask ME, and no one else. I'll have one radio in my team on Company TAC 2 at all times. No one else knows about this radio channel but us, the frequency is VHF 51.125. I don't give a fuck about my career, so this shit can all fall on me. Besides, once we leave Shitghanistan and hand this land back over to the Afghan Army, they're gonna get slaughtered by the Taliban, and everything we did will be a fuckin waste anyways, so if we lose a couple hearts and minds it really doesn't fuckin' matter. This country's fucked. So let's just make it home alive. Are we fuckin' clear?"

I will never, until the day I die, give a better, more uplifting, more boner creating, motivational speech, than I did in front of those Sergeants.

I've said it before and I'll say it again, I was a terrible officer, and it's for the better that I got medically retired before I carried on belligerently the way I did. I've never been good with authority, but in the Marine Corps, I actually had less respect for authority than I ever did in my life. This is a pretty shameful thing for an officer to say, but if you can't tell already, I won't write bullshit. I write the truth, and the truth is I was a belligerent bastard. For all the future officers reading this, don't be like me, guys, it's not a good way to be if you're into career advancement, good FITREPS, and medals. There are plenty of other books written for young officers to teach you how to be good, well-behaved officers, and this book ain't one of 'em.

Oh, and for the record, Fox Company didn't kill a single civilian, not FUCKING ONE, and that's documented by battalion battle records. During the course of the deployment, we were rained on by IEDs, RPGs, machine gun fire, mortars, and rocks, and throughout all that, we applied medical care to hundreds of people, and saved at least a few dozen Afghan lives with our medevacs. Not a single civilian was hurt by us, and we dropped a lot of bombs, shot a lotta shit, and most importantly, and most gratifyingly, we killed a ton of Taliban.
Not too shabby if you ask me.

Lance Corporal Denver Short

Job:
0311 Rifleman

Unit:
3rd Battalion, 6th Marines

Battlefields Fought on:
Marjah, Helmand Province, Afghanistan

Insert: April 28, 1989
Extract: August 29, 2012

Method:
Self-inflicted GSW to the head

Text a bro,

"Be honest bro, if there were no women left in the world would you fuck a chai boy? And before you bullshit me, I would have a fucking HAREM of them. Ok your turn!"

These journal entries were written on the morning and evening of Operation Branding Iron 2.1A. I still cannot believe what a fucking nutcase I was as I headed into this operation. There is no better word than IRREVERENT to describe this journal entry, and me in general.

Actual Journal Entry,

1000, July 5, 2012
Platoon Cmdr/Platoon Sergeant tent, FOB Shirgazi, Musa Quala District, Helmand Province, Afghanistan

SO, it's 1000 and we leave for our mission in about 13 hours. We are going to be picked up by helicopters for this one, and dropped into the middle of a fucking hornet's nest of Taliban, into an area controlled by the Taliban, with their own gov't, courts, jails, you name it. If you aren't Taliban, you're a Taliban sympathizer. So basically, I expect this Op to be fucking wild.

What does that mean for Donny? It means I'm excited out of my mind, blaring David Guetta's new album, dancing all over the staff and officer tent while I pack my bag for the Op. It was like before football games, and before fun trips with friends back home. It has the same energy and excitement for me. Luckily, Boden was just as excited as me, as he always gets before combat operations. The shittier and more dangerous it is, the more excited and happy he gets. We are identical in that sense. We keep making jokes about getting up on rooftops and shooting all the weapon systems that we have. We joked about how many of the cockroaches we would kill and from how far. I looked over at Captain

Black, callsign "Ogre," a badass cobra pilot who also did MMA, and saw that he was not amused nor excited in the slightest. I turned my music down and said,

"Hey Ogre, I know how excited you are, so I'm going to make sure you are a part of our pre-combat-choreographed dance. I always choreograph a little dance before each operation that expresses the emotions we are feeling." Boden found it hysterical, as did I.

Ogre, who is on his fifth combat deployment, says with a very serious face,

"The only pre-combat thing I do before missions is pray to God that I come back with everything I left with."

I paused for a split second, then yelled "LAAAAAAAAME" and turned my music up and went back to dancing to David Guetta.

After I had already begun dancing, I thought about how rude it was of me to yell "LAME" to Ogre. Then I thought, *ehhhh, he's a Cobra pilot, he's been more scared before*.

2200

Its time. Bout to put my gear on and head to the LZ to get picked up by the helicopters. I think the fear will set in right as the birds show up, and will last until we get into our first compound. This is gonna be a good one…

Corporal Adam Wolfel

Jobs:
0311 Rifleman & 0331 Machine Gunner

Units:
2nd Battalion, 8th Marines & 3rd Battalion, 6th Marines

Battlefields Fought on:
Marjah, Helmand Province, Afghanistan

Insert: February 14, 1991
Extract: December 13, 2014

Method of extract:
Self-inflicted GSW to the head

Message a battle buddy right now,

"Hey bro, not to be gay or anything but can you please suck my dick?"

"LIEUTENANT O'MALLEY, SIR, THE BIRDS ARE INBOUND!"

Weird and shitty things happen in combat. A lot of times you react on instinct. My instincts are usually disgusting and perverted.

THE SHACK

2230, July 5, 2012
3rd Porta Potty on the left nearest the LZ, FOB Shirgazi, Musa Quala District, Helmand Province, Afghanistan

I sat on the shitter in disbelief. I had been fantasizing about this operation for over two weeks, and up until that moment, it was the most exciting time of my entire life. But as I dozed off on the shitter, with my pants around my ankles, succumbing to the food poisoning that was tearing through my body and mind, I couldn't get excited about anything. Everything was drained from me, and all I wanted to do was close my eyes and lay down. I finally closed my eyes with my head in my hands, and it felt amazing. Despite the fact that I had great sleep for the last several days, my body was begging me to shut down. I thought about the food I ate three hours prior. It was spaghetti with meat sauce, peaches, and fried chicken. Nothing about the meal seemed more terrible than any other meal. There was no additional foul odor, it wasn't sitting out in the heat for too long as far as I could tell, and it seemed in general, decently fit for mammal consumption.

I had to fight it. I knew I couldn't let the poisoning get the best of me and ruin my ability to rack up a ton more kills on the last combat operation of my deployment. I started slapping myself, pinching myself, mumbling "FUCK YOU" to myself, and when I noticed there was a bottle of water on the ground, I poured the bottle on my head knowing damn well it could have been someone else's piss. Nothing worked, so finally I did what every Marine does when he can't stay awake: I grabbed my dick and started jerking myself off. I tried thinking of the blonde female reporter, but it was a hard sell and only created minimal blood flow. I tried thinking about my drop dead gorgeous ex-gf and I got some more blood flow, but it wasn't enough. I ran every porn in my computer through my head as fast as I could until I got to a three-way-cougar porn with Lisa Ann that brought immediate blood flow to my dick. I started a good rhythm until I felt a wicked pain in my stomach that made me almost keel over. All blood flow to my dick was rerouted to my stomach, the remaining blood in my brain was drained out, and I fell asleep on the shitter with my dick halfway hard, with my head in my hands, and looking like I was crying, right before a helo raid. Again, I feel the need to reiterate that I was a Marine infantry officer.

As expected, I started dreaming.

I dreamt that I was on the LZ, sitting on my pack and staring up at the helicopters as they touched down. I heard guys yelling, but I couldn't make out the words. The yelling continued, and almost sounded familiar, but not familiar enough to wake me out of my dream. It almost sounded like someone was telling me that the birds were inbound. I heard someone's name, and then "The birds are inbound!" I thought to myself, *Duh, no shit, I can see them jackass!* The cloud of dust made by the helicopters got bigger until I was engulfed in it, and then everything went black.

The yelling got louder, and closer. I heard banging off in the distance. *Who the fuck is banging,* I thought. *Goddamn! Why can't these fuckin nerds let me sleep?*

Finally, I was awoken by the sound of a Marine banging on my wooden bathroom door and screaming, "LIEUTENANT O'MALLEY, SIR, THE BIRDS ARE INBOUND!"

I snapped up, eyes almost popping out of my head, and heart beating out of my chest, and yelled "ROGER I'M OSCAR MIKE!" I opened the door before I could pull my pants up. The Marine was already gone, so he didn't see me, but I saw a stream of piss squirt out just as I went to stuff my dick back in my pants. I ran back to my pack next to my Fire Support Team and heard Lieutenant Boden yell, "Where the fuck were you?"

"I was on the shitter. Somethin's up, I think I got food poisoning."

"Well they've been looking for you for like five minutes. Lemme guess, Don, you tryin' to throw one last beat before you get your dick blown off?"
He said it with a tilted head, indicating he knew I was busted.

"Yeah, pretty much." I said.

"You were!" He said excitely, "fuckin' scumbag!"

"Shut the fuck up and remember to lean to the left when your bird goes down asshole." I convinced him before every helo Op that his bird was going down.

"You wish, bitch. See you in hell." He turned to walk back to his platoon.

"You can go to hell, bro, I'll be in Valhalla with the rest of the Marines." I said it as I put my pack on, without looking at him. I don't think he heard me.

My radio operator, Lance Corporal Cox, helped me with my pack, as he always did because of my pathetic shoulders.

"Damn sir, you outdid yourself this time," Cox said in his Mississippi accent, referring to the weight of my pack. We were in frequent competition to carry more weight.

"Yeah, someone's gotta carry the weight of this team." I said it with extreme arrogance and he smiled, because I frequently bragged about being able to manhandle more weight than everyone else. Little did he know that thanks to the food poisoning, I felt weaker than I had the entire deployment, and was being crushed under the weight of my pack. I felt like a total bitch.

Squealing under the weight of my pack, I watched in awe as the first wave of birds landed on our LZ. I always looked at Marine helicopters like they were angels, or Gods, or something magical. My eyes followed the birds all the way down to the deck. A minute later I walked with my squad onto the bird, feeling completely numb. I got buckled in and counted everyone else who came on the bird. I thought I'd be scared by that point, but I wasn't.

I figured the fear would set in just before we landed, as it usually did. Maybe it was the food poisoning, maybe it was my inability to take serious shit seriously; whatever the fuck it was, I wasn't scared, and that felt weird. I rehearsed the insert plan in my head, and looked at my map one last time before we headed into the fire.

Corporal Clay Hunt

Job:
0311 Rifleman and 0317 Scout Sniper

Unit:
2nd Battalion, 7th Marines

Battlefields Fought On:
Fallujah, Al Anbar Province, Iraq
Sangin, Helmand Province, Afghanistan

Insert: April 18, 1982
Extract- March 31, 2011

Method of extract:
Self-inflicted GSW to the head

Text a battle buddy right now,

"Wanna go shoot guns and fuck?"

"FUCK THAT MUTHERFUCKER, I swear on everything I believe in that if he was here with us on this operation I would end his fucking life and save the rest of the battalion from his selfishness, and more importantly, from the pain of watching someone pin a Bronze Star on his fucking chest. I could reduce suffering for an entire Marine Infantry Battalion with one snap of his skinny little fucking neck."

The parasite that ate through my insides put my mind in a dark place. A place so dark I hope I never go there again. A place so dark it's dangerous, because some people who go there get lost and never come back.
It takes years to feel normal again after this shit.

The New York Philharmonic

2255, July 5, 2012
Stick 2, Wave 1, HMH 466- Wolfpack, 7000 ft. above sea level, Lwar Bajigar, Zamindawar District, Helmand Province, Afghanistan

The sound of the CH-53's engines drowned out the sounds of life. All that was left was a loud whirring sound and the chopping of the big blades through the Afghan sky. The Marines on the bird were quiet. There were no jokes nor smiles, not even from me.
I once asked Marines what they were thinking about as we flew in to a raid. I heard the responses: "my wife," "my children," "my family," "praying to God," and "blah blah fucking blah." I stopped listening because I couldn't fucking understand it.

All I could think about while on the helos was taking contact upon insert, immediate actions, machine guns, explosions, hurt Marines in need of medevac, which Marines I thought might act like pussies, which guys I could count on to be cool, and of course, dead bodies. Mounds of dead Taliban bodies with me hysterically laughing over them with my rifle in one hand, and my kabar in the other, ready to cut their fucking ears off to make the ear necklace I'd been dreaming about since I was a kid.

I never once thought about home, mom, dad, friends, nothing.... I could give a fuck less about them while I'm flying into a raid. That's just what I need right? To think about my parents and get all emotional when I've got a big job to do? Fuck no. I'm a soft-hearted-ball-of-mush deep down, and in Afghanistan, that ball of mush was suppressed so hard it took over a year for my cold stone heart to turn soft and warm again. Hell, to this day I'm still trying to unfuck the rewiring that occurred in my brain during combat. Anyways, fuck that emo shit.

The crew chiefs gave the hand signal, "two minutes."
Everybody passed the word down the line by holding two fingers up and yelling in the guys' ear next to them, "TWO MINUTES." I don't know why we even bothered yelling.
I looked out the back of the bird as the ramp lowered and I was able to see the terrain we were landing on. It looked just like rest of the Helmand Province- a dry, barren, pre-historic, worthless, shithole.
As I studied the Afghan countryside I anticipated the moment that the fear would make me shake. I knew the

shakes wouldn't last long, but I had come to expect them for a brief second.

My jaw tightened up slightly and my heart rate speed up a little, but the fear wasn't even close to what I expected. Thanks to the parasite that was tearing through my body, the only things I felt were the knife in my stomach, full body weakness, and a general inability to give fucks.

I rehearsed in my head my immediate action if we took contact in the middle of the large dirt field that we were getting dropped into.

I'd take cover behind a pebble and then low crawl next to my radio operator Cox, who would be setting up the satellite antenna, assuming of course that he wasn't shot. I'd get on the hook with battalion and tell them to fire on all my priority targets. Dafflitto, my JTAC, would already begin a nine line directing Close Air Support onto the buildings surrounding us. I never needed to say much to Dafflitto, he was always ready to slay bodies.

I knew that battalion would demand to know the civilian situation on, and around the buildings I was calling-for-fire on. If they thought there MIGHT be the potential for civilian casualties, they wouldn't give clearance to drop any bombs or do anything fun.

So instead of wasting valuable time, I would lie like a salesman who needed just ONE more sale to win Salesman of the Year and get the promotion he'd been dreaming of. This is what I was prepared to say to battalion.

"Warcross this is Fox Fires, I have solid eyes on all three targets and they are clearly empty compounds. What I'm seeing confirms our reconnaissance. All three compounds are bombed out and are completely devoid of civilian life. I have eyes on muzzle flashes coming from murder holes in all three compound walls. We are pinned down, and I can see the enemy maneuvering on us. Requesting immediate and emergency CAS and conventional artillery fire missions on priority targets AB1003……"

Basically, a SOLID fucking lie that would have gotten the job done.
What about civilian casualties, you may ask? Bitch please. I got a better question, what about Marine casualties?
At that point in time, the word "civilians" was synonymous with "zero fucks."

With my "immediate action lie" ready to rock and roll, I watched the ground get closer to us at an alarming speed. We were hovering and descending, and at any moment we'd touch down. I took my body weight off the seat and flexed my legs just in case we had a hard landing. My back didn't appreciate hard landings.
The landing turned out to be very gentle. The ramp lowered all the way down, allowing the rear crew chief to run out to the tail and remind us to exit the bird to the left. If you run to the right out of a CH-53, you deserve to be eliminated from the gene pool.

I stood up, as did everyone, and checked my gear. Then I turned on my thermal optic so that I had an excuse to call for fire on the first heat signature that wasn't a Marine. If the first heat signature was a baby chicken, too bad. It should have known better than to be a baby chicken in the Helmand Province that night.

It's thoughts like this that cause guys to feel different when they come home.

The helo was supposed to land with the nose pointed north, which meant that as we exited the back of the bird and turned left we were going to face east. Our objective was south, and we could expect contact from the west. Those who understand common sense tactics can see the problem here. It was whatever.

If the helo was NOT going to land with the nose pointed north, the crew chiefs would tell us the new nose direction. They said nothing, which meant we were landing pointing north, and I could expect to be shot in the back upon insert.

It was whatever.

I turned my NVG's on and dropped them over my left eye. Immediately I was reminded that my NVG's sucked more asshole than a two girls one cup video, so I lifted them right back up and turned it off. It was whatever.

My Fire Support Team was in the middle of the bird, so we exited just behind our security team. Guys always do this little half-jog-half-walk thing when they insert and extract, but it's usually not needed unless you're under fire or in a huge hurry. A half jog with 120 pounds on your back is the same speed as my Grandma walking to the couch.

As we walked east and got into our security position I finally woke the fuck up, but I didn't get scared. It was weird, I felt numb. I'm embarrassed to say I was *hoping* we got shot at so I could start wasting everything around me.

We waited in our security 360 until we had radio checks and made sure no idiots forgot anything, then we got up and headed to our first compound. With the helicopters gone, it was eerily quiet. I looked all around me and appreciated the scene. The terrain looked exactly like I imagined. It was perfectly flat, dry, dusty terrain, with compounds spaced randomly and at least 500 meters apart, leaving large open danger areas that are perfect for enemy machine gunners. Rusty old power lines ran through the town and hung dangerously low. My battalion lost one Marine to power lines, and the unit we replaced lost two Marines to power lines. Power lines were not our friends.

We were in a large dust cloud created by the helos and there were four long lines of Marines walking quietly through the dust to their next position. The squad with the breaching team was headed directly to the objective, which was compound 34. They were going to make entry, and the rest of us were going to hold security and wait while they blew their way in.

We were walking at about .5 miles per hour, and for the first time in my life I thought I was going to fall out. I was being smothered by my stupid pack, and I became convinced that I was a chick trying to make it in the grunts. Here's why;

Before we stepped off on the operation, I waited for everyone else to weigh their packs, and saw that I had to break 89 pounds to have the heaviest pack out of all the Officers and Staff NCOs. I walked into second platoon's tent and said, "Who want's to give up some ammo?" Within milliseconds I had 400 rounds of machine gun ammo and 4 mortar rounds in my hands, bringing my pack to a solid 93 pounds. This was in addition to the 60 pounds of body armor and ammo I had on my body. This proved to be retarded and made me feel like far less than a man.

To top it off, I was being degraded by the parasite that lived inside me. It was laughing at me, and telling me that I was a fucking bitch who couldn't hack it in the grunts.

"You're a fucking BITCH O'Malley! You think you're cool cuz you're a grunt? You ain't no grunt! You're a fuckin' bitch! FUCK you and yo muthafuckin' mama, you ain't got shit on me you fucking pussy-ass, ZERO!"

I was tempted to turn my rifle on my own stomach and pull the trigger on burst, just to shut that fucking parasite up forever.

It's thoughts like this that cause guys to feel different when they get home.

We finally got to our spot and waited for the breaching team to make a hole. I heard some radio traffic about the entry, "Six, this is two, it looks like the last unit here blew a huge hole for entry, we're gonna blow another hole   right   next   to   it."

"Two, this is six, I copy, already an entry. Can we sweep the entry and use it without blowing another one?"

All of a sudden my pain went away, my face got hot, and

my blood boiled. *USE AN EXISTING ENTRYWAY! AT NIGHT!?!? ARE WE FUCKING RETARDED?*

Let me explain the two golden rules in Shitghanistan.

1) Don't go in compounds that Marines have already been in. They have IEDs.

2) Don't use entryways that Marines have already walked through. They have IEDs.

My brain couldn't understand why we were walking into a compound that Marines had been in prior, through the SAME entryway that Marines had already entered through. Then magically I could understand, because I remembered that the battalion commander had created a policy of "minimizing collateral damage" by not blowing our way into compounds if we didn't HAVE to. He applauded commanders for "finding an alternate way without inflicting more discomfort on the Afghan people." As if their mud walls were so fuckin' expensive….

The thought of the BC saying those words made me clinically insane. My body shook with anger as I thought to myself, *FUCK THAT MUTHERFUCKER, I swear on everything I believe in that if he was here with us on this operation I would end his fucking life and save the rest of the battalion from his selfishness, and more importantly, from the pain of watching someone pin a Bronze Star on his fucking chest. I could reduce suffering for an entire Marine Infantry Battalion with one snap of his skinny little fucking neck.*

Thoughts of the ways I would kill him raced through my mind like a porn video. Thoughts of murder turned my anger to happiness, my body relaxed, and of course, I fell asleep in the dirt next to a compound wall. At least I had a smile on my face.

I dreamt of choking the BC with my bare hands while he was taking a shit. I could hear him squealing as he tried to get out of my death grip, I could feel him tapping out, and in my little fantasy, I looked him in his eyes and saw terrible fear. The same fear that hundreds of his Marines had as they walked through bomb alleys, the same fear that hundreds of Marines had in their eyes as they laid on the ground bleeding out, wondering if this was the end- while their buddies turniqueted them and tried to save them. I saw that same fear in his eyes, and it made me happy. I choked until I felt him go limp, and I smiled as I watched the life leave his body. Then I spat in his face and considered leaving my next diarrhea shit on it.

Remember those sniper's who pissed on the dead Taliban? Yeah, those guys were fucking amateurs, I would of projected diarrhea all over those Taliban, then lit em' on fire.

But that's just me. Call me old fashioned.

It's thoughts like this that cause guys to feel different when they get home.

All of a sudden something hit my leg, and I looked down. In real life, someone kicked me and said, "Sir, get up."

I opened my eyes and gasped for breath, because apparently I was holding my breath as I fantasized about killing the BC. I relaxed the death grip I had on myself and looked up, it was my Radio Operator, Lance Corporal Cox. He held out his hand to help me up.

I mumbled "Fuck you," as I rolled onto my knees, and then stood myself up- knowing damn well there wasn't a Marine in the Company who could've picked my heavy ass off the ground.

Cox said sarcastically in his Mississippi accent, "Ya know, I got feelings too sir, I know you think I'm some Viking war God, but I'm just a man sir. Just a man, and your words   can   hurt   sometimes."

I smiled on the inside, because I was too miserable to smile on the outside. Come to think of it just about every time Cox opened his hick mouth I smiled on the inside and the outside, but that was because I loved him so damn much.

We resumed walking towards the objective compound, and I tried not to collapse. Like a true bitch.

I heard over the radio that 2nd platoon was done sweeping the entryway for IEDs and was making entry into the compound. I got tense as I waited to hear the sound of someone popping an IED. I woke up and became more alert, finally I could see Marines walking through the entryway, and it made me almost shit my pants. It looked exactly like the last time a few Marines walked through a hole in a wall and popped an IED, sending a pair of legs flying past the whole squad. One of the legs whizzed by my Marine's face. He was a little messed up in the head after that.

I watched a few dozen Marines walk through the hole as I waited in line and inched closer. I really didn't give a fuck if I got blown up. Hell, if I got blown up that meant

I'd get to take my stupid fucking pack off, I'd get to lie down, and I'd get some morphine.

If I died, I'd take a dirt nap and I'd be somebody else's fuckin'   problem.

I just really didn't wanna see anyone else blow up. That's annoying.

I took my turn through the hole, as did everyone else, without incident. The entire company ended up consolidating in that giant compound and posting security on the rooftops as we waited till daylight to see if the Taliban wanted to come out and play.

0800, July 6, 2012
Compound 34, Zulu Sector, Lwar Bajigar, Zamindawar
District, Helmand Province, Afghanistan

That day was the hottest day of my entire life. My team
and I made shade out of a tarp that got so hot I burned
my head on it. The parasite in my intestines was
growing, and was eating more of me. I was passing in
and out of consciousness as I tried to battle track the
company's movements, and I was becoming
progressively more worthless as a Marine officer. Finally
it got so bad I tapped out. I turned to my Arty FO and
mumbled, "Bro, I'm fucking garbage. Take the map and
the radio, you're the boss."
He said, "Don't worry dude, I got you. Just drink some
fuckin water would you? You look like death."
I grunted as I fell over, too weak to flip him a bird, and
sipped a bottle of water that was on the ground next to
me. It was so fucking hot that it literally burnt my mouth
and esophagus. I stopped drinking water- as I melted in
the Afghan sun, and that proved to be a very poor
decision.
The Taliban didn't come, so I spent the entire day barely
conscious, melting in the Afghan sun.

We moved to another compound at night, under the
cover of darkness, taking advantage of the fact that the
Taliban enjoyed sleep just as much as the rest of the
third world.

0200, July 7, 2012
Compound 13, Zulu Sector, Lwar Bajigar, Zamindawar District, Helmand Province, Afghanistan

This is the compound that my team holed up in for the rest of the operation. In my compound were headquarters platoon and 1st platoon. 2nd platoon and 3rd platoon took over a couple compounds a few hundred meters away on either side of my compound, creating a company triangle defense. It worked out pretty well.

Sniper 1A and Sniper 1B were forward with 2nd and 3rd platoons respectively, and 2nd platoon had a mortar tube run by Corporal Delawder. The only time Delawder ever seemed mentally stimulated was when he was firing mortars, and he was damn good at it.

My compound had the Radio Battalion guys, one mortar tube run by Corporal Crosson, and my bestie, Sergeant Loya.

One of the cool things about being a Fire Support Team Leader in Afghanistan was the outstanding amount of aircraft we had on station. There were very few hours in the day that we did not have some form of aerial reconnaissance at our disposal, and since aerial recon was our most effective way of hunting these cockroaches, we enjoyed every second of it. Sergeant Dafflitto had a sweet optical device that clipped onto his sunglasses and allowed him to see what the pilots were seeing. It looked like high speed Special Forces gear, and in addition to working perfectly, it eliminated the need to carry the heavy-ass Toughbook laptop and all the giant batteries needed to power it. We took turns using the high-speed device to recon the area, and as expected, we saw the same thing we always saw when we got dropped into Taliban country.

Trucks and vans several kilometers away filled with middle aged males, moved from building to building, picking up more guys who carried bags big enough to fit guns in, from the building to the vehicle, and then headed our way.

You would think that after seeing this exact same thing all deployment we'd have enough evidence to drop bombs on these assholes before they ever got into position to attack us, but no, they *could* be civilians.

FML.

So we sat there watching those pieces of shit maneuver on us and get into positions to attack us. My team relayed their movements to the rest of the company so that we'd all be ready.

By around noon on July 7 the Taliban kicked off the party with a couple well placed shots at our rooftop security. The rooftop machine gunners identified a couple shitheads and opened up on them. The Taliban responded by opening up with machine guns from at least three different positions and lobbed a few RPGs at us.

Game fucking on.

My compound erupted into a concert of Marine Corps awesomeness. Everybody tightened up, got their edges back, and got ready for battle. The machine gunners were doling out hate and discontent at the rapid rate, and the mortar men prepared to shred bodies into jelly.

The sounds of machine guns blaring, radios crackling, Marines yelling out enemy positions, Marines yelling for more ammo, mortars firing, enemy bullets snapping overhead, planes flying, and bombs exploding- was like the New York Philharmonic playing their final concert during a fireworks show. The machine guns and M16s were the woodwinds, the mortars, RPGs, and 203s were the percussions, the Marines communicating to each other were the brass, and the radio traffic made up the strings. The way each individual instrument blended together was magical. It made me want to get dressed up in my blues and take my ex-gf to a rooftop to watch the greatest show on earth. I wouldn't even ask her for a BJ, I'd be content just holding her hand for the duration of the show.

The Marine Corps symphony of death filled my heart and soul with unconditional love and joy, and my dick with blood.

I might sound a little crazy, some might even call me psychotic, but I'm really not. I'm what the Marine Corps needed me to be to ensure I was better at killing the enemy than they were at killing us. Every other guy who ever loved being at war shouldn't feel weird, crazy, nor different. We were what our country needed us to be. Don't ever forget that.

Immediately I was rejuvenated, and the parasite in my belly became a mere background noise. I got on my radio and understood the battlefield better than anything I've understood in my life. I was in communication with Radio Battalion (RadBn) so they could point their little scanner in each direction that we identified a middle-aged-male. If RadBn got an ICOM signal from the direction that a middle-aged-male was standing and looking at us, I'd have enough evidence to assume that the dude was bad- even if he wasn't shooting at us- and waste him. I was in a frenzy to clear other guys to fire, to direct mortars on targets, to de-conflict with our aerial recon (jets and Predators), and to hear from Dafflitto what the pilots were seeing so that we could stay on top of guys who we once saw shoot at us. It was a fun and exciting game that the Taliban were actually pretty good at.

The Taliban knew our rules of engagement and knew that they could get away with murder. They could have one guy pulling a trigger from behind a murder hole, then another guy could stand right next to the hole and spot the rounds for the machine gunner. Our legal ability to shoot the spotter was a grey area according to the CO. According to me, the spotter's a dead man. The Taliban could stage an RPG in a field and casually walk over to it. Then they could fire it, put it back down, and hide. If we saw them hours later (according to orders from higher) we wouldn't be able to kill them.
Fortunately for Fox Company, I was never very good at following orders.

If a Marine said, "sir, I think this guy shot at us earlier...."
My response was always, "well then why fuck isn't he dead yet?"

That was fun.
Unfortunately, I will never be that cool again, and just thinking about it makes me sad.

0450, July 8, 2012
Compound 13, Zulu Sector, Lwar Bajigar, Zamindawar District, Helmand Province, Afghanistan

Reveille.

The company had not moved since we entered compound 13. Our mission was "to disrupt Taliban operations," and our presence in Lwar Bajigar was doing exactly that. The Taliban had been coming to us, and we had been picking them off like rabbits in the backyard, so there was no need for us to move compounds and risk popping an IED. Gotta give credit to the CO for that one. As much as I've hated on him, the decision not to move compounds in Lwar Bajigar undoubtedly kept a few more legs attached to our guys.

The reveille call was really annoying because I was getting great quality sleep on one of the bright colored Afghan mattress pads. To this day, I have never slept more soundly than I did on those pads. At reveille we weren't getting shot at, we had no air on station, and had not identified any targets. Therefore, I saw no reason for anyone to wake me up. I wanted to sleep until the Taliban wanted to play, then I wanted to wake up and resume the symphony of death. Again, terrible officer.

I got up, but I wasn't happy about it.

A few hours later the Taliban came out of the woodwork with a chip on their shoulder. It might have been because the day before, a few Sergeants wasted a couple guys in a field a few hundred meters away, and then did reenactments of the way the shitheads died immediately after. It was pretty hilarious, and if the Taliban saw, I could understand why they'd be pissed.

The whole operation had been a fairytale up till that point, full of weapons employment, laughter, and killing. With less than 18 hours left to slay bodies in Afghanistan, we were all determined to keep it a fairytale, because if one dude got hurt, it would be a total buzz kill, and all of a sudden war wouldn't seem like so much fun, for a few days....

I sat behind a pillar with my Fire Support Team and starting plotting targets on my map. The Taliban had us surrounded pretty good, and were firing from at least 6 different positions. Our machine guns were rockin' and rollin' and we had mortars firing every few minutes. The New York Philharmonic continued another fine performance.

2nd platoon commander Boden was dropping mortars on a couple of enemy machine gunners about a kilometer away, and making less than 30 mil adjustments, which I thought were a little silly at first. I listened to his radio traffic as he made his corrections and I lost my patience. I was about to butt in and say, "Bro, it's an AREA fire weapon, you don't need to make those tiny corrections." Just before I opened my mouth over the radio, he said in a monotone, professional voice, "The last round landed on their heads with an above ground burst." Then a few seconds later he got back on the net and said with excitement, "that was awesome."

I didn't see it, but everyone who did, said it was absolutely beautiful. Boden's employment of the mortars was like a shaky violin solo performance that ended with a flawless finale, complete with drums and cymbals.

Doc Belford walked around checking on guys like the good Corpsman that he was, and noticed the intense loss of color in my face and weird swings of consciousness. "You doin' ok sir?"

"Yeah, better than ever Doc."

"You don't look too hot sir."

"I didn't get to do my hair this morning, exCUUUUSE me."

He laughed and told me he was gonna give me an IV bag of fluid. I told him I didn't want it, because I'd never forgive myself if someone else got shot or blown up and died because we were out of fluid. Doc assured me he had enough, and stuck me with the IV. Thank God he did, because I ended up sucking down three bags faster than he'd ever seen. My stupid ass would have been a heat case for the first time in my life had I waited any longer.

The machine gunners and mortar gunners were constantly yelling for more ammo as they fired everything they had at the Taliban who surrounded us. This was the cue for guys like me, who carried extra ammo, to hand it over to the guys who were pulling triggers. Unfortunately for me, there were lots of guys who carried extra ammo and wanted to get rid of it. So as the ammo-men ran around collecting ammo, everyone who had ammo held it up in the air for the ammo-men to see. I was so desperate to reduce the weight in my pack that I snapped at one of the ammo-men who was about to grab machine gun ammo from someone else.

"HEY MUTHERFUCKER RIGHT HERE!" He didn't hear me so I yelled again, "GARCIA, I'm fucking talking to you!"

He looked over at me scared and said, "YES SIR!" I said, "take my muthafuckin' link before you take anyone else's." Officership at its finest.
"Roger that sir," he said and ran over.

"That one right there killer," I said pointing to my pack. "I think I got four hundred rounds in there."

"Roger sir."

I kept one eye on my map and one eye on him as he went through my pack. I saw him grab 200 rounds and start to turn away. The Marine in me wanted to keep my mouth shut and suck it up. The little bitch in me wanted him to take all 400 rounds and lighten my load a bit more. I tried hard to keep my mouth shut, but the little bitch inside me took over. Just as he started walking away I did the unthinkable.

"Whoa, whoa, did you take them all?"

"No sir, I only needed—"

"Garcia get those fucking rounds out of my pack."

"Roger that sir."

My ego is still recovering from that.

In the middle of very intense fighting we took contact from a few compounds 700m north east of our position. Loya identified the targets and called them in, but I was busy so I didn't hear them.

I was focused on a few other targets that I was directing mortars onto, while Dafflitto ran up a nine line to a Harrier for a gun run. With me being too busy to direct a weapons system onto Loya's targets, Loya took it upon himself to grab an AT-4 and clear a back blast area in preparation to fire it.

I got a call on the radio to fire asking for permission to fire the AT-4.

"Fires, this is 3-Charlie, request permission to employ the AT-4 at an enemy machine gunner, our back blast area is all clear."

"Standby 3-Charlie, what's your target?"

He hesitated, "Compound tw- twenty."

I checked my map and noticed the compound was over 700m away, well out of the max effective range of the AT-4. I got confused. So I clarified, "3-Charlie, say again compound number"

"Compound 20."

I responded quickly, "Ok are you dumb or just an asshole?"

As it turns out, they had a GoPro filming the whole thing, and the look of disappointment in Loya's face when he got denied was hysterical. On the video Loya said, "fuck dude, I don't wanna carry this fuckin' shit back home."

Corporal Crosson, the head mortarman in my compound, heard that there were a couple of middle aged males who appeared to be spotting us from compound 21. Taking initiative, he sighted his mortar tube on compound 21, then ran over to me and said, "Lieutenant O'Malley sir, I'm ready to fire on compound 21."

I said, "Well fuck man, I don't have confirmation from RadBn that those guys are bad."

He hung his head in disappointment. I felt bad, I knew he wanted to squash those guys, but since they weren't holding weapons it was tough to justify killing them while my company commander was around. Not wanting to see my Marine disappointed, I got back on my radio and asked Gunny to tell me the numbers of all buildings he *thought* we were taking fire from. If Gunny *thought* that enemy fire was coming from the same compound that two guys were "looking" at us, that was enough for me to feel good about turning them into pink mist.

"7, this is Fires."

"Go for 7."

"I need the numbers of every compound you think we've taken fire from today."

"Roger Fires, I've got compound 31, 35, 30, 25, and uhhhh, break"

Crosson and I looked at each other like two kids who were hoping dad agreed to take them out for ice cream.

"Compound 24, 23, and uhhh, ummmmm, compound 21, how copy?"

I looked at Crosson with a huge smile on my face and said, "Fire on 21, WASTE THOSE MUTHERFUCKERS." I could see his soul fill with joy.

He ran back to his mortar tube and delivered those scumbags from evil. His first rounds were on target, the two guys who were "looking" at us turned to pink mist and began the afterlife.

To this day I have severe PTSD from the fact that I did NOT get to watch those shitheads die. Enemy Death (ED) makes me happy. Watching ED *as it happens* gives me a huge boner that can only go away with a combat wack.

The combat footage can be seen on my website, donnyomalley.com, and also on the San Diego Union Tribune's website.
http://www.utsandiego.com/news/2012/jul/14/marines-confront-afghan-enemy-in-firefight/

We spent the rest of the day helping a few more Taliban start the afterlife early.

Although this always seemed like we were doing the Taliban a huge favor, because Afghanistan was a fucking shithole that even the animals didn't want to live in. So sending guys to the afterlife, where they supposedly had 70 fresh, untouched pussies waiting for them, was actually a very kind gesture.

The USA is seriously the nicest country in the world...... I digress.

The next story begins at the end of the operation, as we waited for helos to extract us from Lwar Bajigar. This is when I continued hunting my most prized kill. The kill that seemed a distant fantasy. The kill that no one believed I would get.

The kill that would make me a legend in Marine folklore.

All I had was hope, and God's will.
Inshallah.

Corporal Elias Reyes

Job:
0351 Assaultman

Unit:
2nd Battalion, 7th Marines

Battlefields Fought On:
Fallujah, Al Anbar Province, Iraq
Sangin, Helmand Province, Afghanistan

Insert: September 29, 1986
Extract: April 12, 2014

Method of extract:
Self-inflicted GSW to the head

Text a bro,

"If you don't text me back I'm gonna nail every one of your ex's and send you the pictures. Wait, you'd probably like that. Just fuckin text me back bitch."

"I was devastated. I thought I was making amazing headway with the reporter, we were getting to know each other on a very personal level, and most importantly, I was forging a deep and soulful connection that would inevitably lead to unprotected sex in an MRAP or porta potty.....I wish more people understood that war is hell."

The presence of a woman is such a powerful force that it can never be underestimated. Women, indirectly, and without knowing it, move the world.

THE HUNT CONTINUES

2300, July 8, 2012
Compound 13, Zulu Sector, Lwar Bajigar, Zamindawar District, Helmand Province, Afghanistan

Fox Company consolidated into the large compound that headquarters and first platoon had been holed up in for the last two days. This was the compound that I had been operating in as I directed fires for the beautiful orchestra of death that is a Company sized battle.
As we waited for a squad to prep the LZ, I saw the reporter sitting on the ground with her arms wrapped around her legs and her notepad in her right hand. She looked like she was getting ready to take a nap. Normal human compassion would have dictated that I left her alone to sleep, but my personal mission to stick my dick in a living human vagina overrode all sense of anything

compassionate. All that remained in my brain was primitive, animalistic instinct.

I knew this was my chance, so I said to my Artillery Lieutenant, "Hey bro, you got the radio, I'm gonna' do WORK." He knew exactly what I was going to do because I made it well known to my team that I was on a mission to nail the reporter. He smiled and said, "good luck Donny."

I walked over and sat down in the dirt next to her. She was to the right of me, and Dafflitto was to the left of me laying flat on his back in the pile of chicken shit that I slept on the night before. Piles of chicken shit are way more comfy than Afghan ground.

"So hayya' doin, Martha?"

She looked at me with a smile, and appeared happy to see me. Her warm smile filled me with hope, and blood flow.

"I'm great, happy everyone's alive and well," she said.

"Well that's good to hear, I like your spirit." I pointed to her as I said, "you've been awfully comfortable on a pretty gnarly combat mission."

"You mean for a girl?" she asked.

"Abso-fucking-lutely for a girl," I looked her right in the eyes as I said it, letting her know I wasn't going to bullshit her, "but more specifically, for a girl who hasn't trained for combat."

"Touché," she said.

She readjusted her position to rest on her left arm and speak to me as she looked over her left shoulder. "Well, I've been combat reporting for a while, and don't get me wrong, I still get scared, but not as much as I used to."

I nodded, pretending to be very interested in her words. Then I asked her a question that I thought was the key to the door of her bedroom.
"So tell me, what made you want to be a combat reporter?"

The question was deep, open ended, and expressed my interest in her feelings and her past. If she actually took the time to answer it, I'd be one step closer to the pussy.

She changed her position again, this time to sit crossed legged Indian style and face me directly. She put her hand to her heart, and spoke passionately.

"Well, I've always been fascinated by the military, and many of the men in my family have served in the Army and Navy, so I thought, you know, it would be fun to report on them." She shrugged. "I kinda felt like I owed it to them to report on them, you know? I felt it was the least I could do for my country, and the men and women who served it. So I started out after college at the beginning of the war in Iraq. I was embedded with Army units for most of my time there, and I loved it. I mean, it was scary, and thrilling, and exciting, and then heartbreaking when soldiers got hurt. I know it's terrible to say, but I felt like I was on the adventure of a lifetime. Then one day we came across a Marine unit in Ramadi who had just come back from really hard fighting. We heard they lost a lot of guys, so we expected them to be sensitive, and we tried to keep our distance. Then as our unit got closer to them, I heard them laughing. They were the most fun and crazy group of men I had ever seen. They were so full of life, confidence, twisted jokes, stories of killing, and some, well, sometimes, oddly intense love for each other; I was just drawn to them, and I knew I had to report on them. I switched out of my Army unit that week, and joined a Marine unit, and I've been with the Marines ever since."

She smiled after that last line, obviously happy with her decision to report on the Marines.

As I listened to her story, my heart swelled with joy, my eyes swelled with tears, and my dick swelled with blood. This woman had just summed up the true beauty and awesomeness of United States Marines in just a few sentences, and not only that, she was attracted to and understood everything that made Marines exceptional. I no longer wanted to simply stick my dick in her, I wanted to make sweet, romantic, passionate love to her, and whisper sweet nothings in her ear as I blew a load in her that was so magnificent, it guaranteed conception, regardless of her menstrual cycle. Then, when I was done making sweet love to her, I would cuddle her, and even offer to pay for Plan B. That's because I'm not only an officer, I'm also a gentleman.

I wanted to lean in and kiss her right then and there; but because I have outstanding discipline that even Carlos Hathcock would admire, I held out.

"Wow, that is out-fucking-standing. You just articulated why Marines are great better than I've ever heard." I shook my head in bewilderment, "Out-standing... So what did you tell the Army when you left?"

"Oh I just told them I wanted to report on the Marines. They were fine. I loved being with the Army too, they were great, but the Marines were just different, as I'm sure you know."

I nodded and smiled. "Right on. So where have you deployed with Marines?"
"Well, I went to Ramadi, Fallujah, Al Hit, pretty much all over the Anbar province, and then I spent 2 months in Sangin with 3/5. "

"Oh shit!" I said.

She raised her eyebrows and said, "Yeah, it took me a while to get over that one."

"I'll bet. Dafflitto was in Sangin with 3/5," I turned and pointed to him. "He saw and did some gnarly shit, and lost a lotta guys. How many guys did you watch blow their fuckin' legs off?"

"More than I ever wanted to."

I shook my head, "Yeah, those guys had it bad. Real bad. I got nothing but the utmost respect for the Sangin guys." I paused for a second and looked at the ground. "Glad you made it back out with the Marines after going through that. You must be pretty fuckin' tough."

"Yeah, you could say so," she paused and looked at the ground, "but not nearly as tough as you guys though."

I smirked, "Well they are," I pointed to the other Marines, "but I'm not tough. I'm actually a huge sopping pussy."

She laughed and waved her hand at me, brushing off my comment, "Yeah, right. All the guys call you the Grim Reaper. I highly doubt you're a pussy."

I shook my head humbly, "No, no, it's all for show. I act like it just to get the guys excited. The young boys are the real bad-asses. They're all my heroes."

"Well isn't that humble of you?" She said.

"What can I say, I'm a humble man."

I thought I heard Dafflitto cough, which made think he was listening to our conversation.

She nodded in thought, clearly attracted to my humility, and finally, like I hoped, she started asking about *me*.

"How about you? Why did you join the Marines?" She asked.

"Well, my dad was a Marine grunt, and without ever saying it, I could feel his love for the Corps. He used to take us to military shows and displays in New York and Washington D.C, you know, when they let families play on the old tanks and helicopters?"

"Oh yeah, of course. I used to love it too," she said.

"Yeah, so the first time I ever played on a helicopter and tank I was hooked. Then in fifth grade art class I drew pictures of skulls on fire, dead bodies, and pictures of battles, while other kids were drawing horses and rainbows. I watched the movie 'Platoon' when I was way too young, and even though it's a tragedy, I fuckin' loved it. There was just no way around it, I had to be a Marine grunt."

"Wow, so it was in you."

"Abso-fuckin-lutely," I nodded. "And after September 11th, when I was a freshman in college, forget it. I was at the recruiters office in a flash, but my dad swore to me that this war was going to last a long time, and he said if combat was what I wanted, I'd still get it after getting my degree. So I finished college, continued partying and traveling like I was gonna die soon, and came to the Marine Corps ready to die with a smile on my face."

"Wow, that's incredible," she said.
She took in every word, and looked at me in deep thought. I hoped that she was imagining my dick inside her. "Is your dad still in the Marines?"

"No, he got out, went to med school, and joined the Navy as a Doctor. He's actually the Director of Medical Services at Balboa Hospital."

"Oh no way, that's so cool! I go there all the time!"

"Yeah it is. One of my buddies got shot, and another blew his leg off a month ago, and my dad went to visit them in their rooms and read them a letter I wrote to them. It was pretty cool. He loves Marines."

She nodded in thought, then asked me the kind of question I was hoping for, the kind of question that insinuated we were connecting on a deep level. The kind of question that leads to penetration.

"Are you close with your father?"

BINGO!
Women are generally attracted to a man who has a good relationship with his parents, it's an indication that he'll be a good father. It's also an indication that it's not as morally wrong to let him insert his good-hearted dick in her good-hearted pussy, without a commitment.

My next line was the truth, and as I said it, I could feel her vagina throb. I scooted closer to her, just for the sake of increasing the emotional impact, and leaned in close.
"I'm INCREDIBLY close with my dad. He knows me better than anyone else on this planet, and not only that, but he's the greatest man I know." I held eye contact as I paused, "If I can be half the man that he is, I'll be happy."

She was so smitten her color changed from white to red. She blushed so hard she started sweating, and her eyes twinkled under the moonlight. I knew the pussy was mine.
She smiled from ear to ear and sounded like a little girl as she said, "do you…..really mean that?"

The way she said it sounded like I just told her that I loved her more than anyone in the whole wide world. It was cute, juvenile, and reaffirmed that I was IN.

Again, I leaned in and looked her deep in the eyes for dramatic effect, "I absolutely mean that. My father's a great man, and I've been incredibly lucky to have him."

"Wow, that's so incredible. Your whole family must be so lucky."

"We certainly are." I nodded as I looked at her with a grin on my face. The grin had nothing to do with my loving family, it was solely derived from the knowledge that I was gonna stick my dick in her.

She continued getting to know me, "so do you have any sibli-"

"FIRST WAVE, ON YOUR FEET," First Sergeant said in less than a yell, but more than a whisper.

I was devastated. I was making amazing headway with the reporter, we were getting to know each other on a very personal level, and most importantly, I was forging a deep and soulful connection that would inevitably lead to unprotected sex in an MRAP or porta potty.
I wish more people understood that war is hell.

I said good-bye, promised her we'd talk later, then got in line, ready to head out of the compound and towards the LZ where we would wait in a ditch for the helicopters to pick us up.

As I stood in line next to Dafflitto, out of earshot of the reporter, I was excited to learn how much of the conversation he heard.

"So, were you taking notes, young Sergeant?" We were the same age but I loved treating him like he was my little brother.

"Notes on what?" He asked.

"Notes on how to fuck pussy! What the fuck do you think?"

"Oh, you mean all that bullshit, weak-ass, faggot game I had to listen to while I was trying to sleep? Yeah I heard it, I literally wanted to throw up in my mouth. I think I did actually."

"WHAT?!" My eyebrows raised to my hairline. "Are you fucking kidding me? That's some SOLID-ass-game, son. I pretty much already laid the pipe."

"You are fucking ridiculous. You literally just sat there and fed her shit, like a trainer feeding a horse carrots. It was fucking disgusting."

"Umm, ACTUALLY, I meant every word, and you KNOW I'm close with my dad, so there was ZERO bullshit in that game." I looked away in disgust, visibly disappointed with his behavior as an NCO.
Dafflitto continued, "Oh, and that shit about you being a humble man, I literally shat myself with laughter."

I smiled, "Ok, so the humble part was a little stretch, but you know I always give credit to you young bucks."

"Ok, maybe you do, I'll give YOU credit for that. But humble? That's the biggest crock of shit I've ever heard in my life," he paused, "and she's not even that hot. I mean, I'd fuck her, but I just don't know what you're getting all hyped up about."

"Dude, are you fucking kidding me!? That's the most beautiful woman I've ever seen in my entire life," I paused for a second, let my eyes drift to the sky, then clarified, "in Afghanistan, right now, in this moment, without pussy for 6 months."

"Yeah, exactly," he said. We both chuckled.

"No, but really," I said, "I see a queen, and I **will** have my queen."

We got the word to head out. We left the safety of the compound, and walked out into the darkness.

Corporal Bradley Coy

Job:
0331 Machine Gunner

Unit:
2nd Battalion, 7th Marines

Battlefields Fought On:
Now Zad, Helmand Province, Afghanistan

Insert: June 8, 1992
Extract: October 25, 2014

Method of Extract:
Self-inflicted GSW to the head

Find a bro on social media and message him right now,

"Hey bro, can you shit on my chest real quick?"

"We looked at each other in silence as our ride out of Taliban Country flew away, leaving us confused and scared in a giant cloud of dust. Our eyes were as wide as they could go, Lt. Godfried looked like he was going to shit himself, Sergeant Dafflitto looked like he was going to vomit, I did shit myself, and in one of the most rare instances in my life, I didn't have a joke; because it was not fucking funny."

There's a saying in the Infantry about helicopters that we say with a smile every time we ride them. The saying is, "Birds go down." I said it a bit more than other guys did, but that's because I'm a twisted little kid that takes everything too far. So why do we say this?
Because birds go down, a lot.

CLOSE CALL

0100, July 9, 2012
LZ Nightowl, Zulu Sector, Lwar Bajigar, Zamindawar District, Helmand Province, Afghanistan

The first wave of Fox Company waited in a ditch that wrapped around a mud compound. We were minutes away from being extracted by CH-53's from a large field that we turned into a landing zone. The ditch was no more than three feet deep and four feet wide. Most guys were on their stomachs and faced the LZ, but some, including myself and Dafflitto, sat up straight on the side of the ditch closest to the wall. I was in charge of the Fire Support Team, and Dafflitto was the JTAC, the guy who controlled all aircraft.

We had been in Zamindawar for three days trying to score a couple more kills in Taliban Country before the war was over for my battalion. It was our last combat mission, and it had been a success, with around 10 enemy kills and no friendly casualties.

For extract, we created an LZ in a large field using Infrared chem lights that could only be seen with Night Vision Goggles. When I say WE, I mean the Sniper Team marked the LZ. It seemed a little odd to have snipers marking the Landing Zone, but at that point, we had come to expect stupid. I didn't know the snipers were marking the LZ, because the company commander didn't tell me. His lack of communication was the source of a lot of ass pain for Fox Company. As I sat in the ditch, I looked through my high speed thermal device and saw some people moving in a tree line about 600 meters away. They were moving slowly, as if they were getting into position, which is what bad guys usually do. I was hungry for some more kills, so I got excited, but I had to check first. I got on the radio,

"All Fox stations, this is Fires, do we have any friendlies on the other side of the LZ, in the tree line?"

"Fires, that's Affirm, we have Sniper 1A at grid 1234576890." It was the CO.

"Roger, that would have been nice to know earlier." I said.

I was a terrible smartass on the radio at times, and I also

lost professional bearing quite frequently. At that point in the deployment we were all very relaxed on the radio, but I was the most unprofessional, stooping so low as to offer prizes over the radio to guys who could find me someone to kill.

"Settle down and stop trying to kill everything, Fires," the CO said. That really fucking pissed me off. It was my last chance to exercise my government granted right to kill enemies of the United States, and I was excited to make a few more bad guys start the afterlife. As a grunt, my CO had no right to speak about killing with a negative tone. I wanted to say, "Don't use my bloodlust as an excuse for your incompetence." But instead I said, "Roger."
My CO and I had a great relationship.

I looked to my right and saw a Marine laying on his stomach with his rifle in front of him. He was so still he looked like he was sleeping, so I looked to my left and saw the same thing. I did a quick scan down the ditch and noticed that everyone looked like they were sleeping. I turned to Dafflitto and said, "how many of these fuckin' assholes do you think are sleeping right now?"

"Pro'lly half of them," he said.

"How much you wanna bet this guy's sleeping?" I said, pointing to the guy to the right of me.

"Who is it?" Dafflitto asked.

"I think that's Jegger," I said.

"Oh he's asleep for sure, I got five on it." Dafflitto was always down to throw 'five on it.'

I turned to Jegger and whispered "Hey, Jegger, Jegger, Jegger, wake the fuck up!"

I looked back at Dafflitto and said, "Yep, he's out." I was too lazy to get up and kick him in his side, so I threw a small rock at him and hit him right in the helmet. He picked his head up with a jolt, indicating that he was just woken up, and looked in both directions.

"Wake the fuck up asshole!" I said.

"I was awake, sir," he said, sounding almost convincing.

"Sure you were, buddy." I nodded sarcastically.
I looked back at Dafflitto, we both smiled and shook our heads, then sat back and admired the silence.

It was one of the most peaceful and relaxing moments I had in all of Afghanistan. Well, it was either that, or I was miserably tired because for the last four days I shat my pants at least 16 times thanks to food poisoning, got less than 6 hours of sleep, and despite sucking down three IV bags, I was still pissing brown.
Or maybe I'm just trying to justify what happened next….

The silence and darkness was a perfect recipe for sleep. I fought hard to stay awake, but sleep was kicking my ass. I tried everything. Pinching myself, slapping myself, asking Dafflitto to punch me, splashing water in my eyes, and finally, thinking about pussy and jerking my dick. I tried thinking about fucking the reporter in an MRAP back on the patrol base, but I couldn't get over the fact that since she was on the operation with us, her pussy probably smelt as bad as my crotch. That thought was a NO-GO for boner time. Instead I thought about my ex-gf who was one of the hottest girls on the planet. Thoughts of being behind her juicy and perfect ass filled my brain, and almost instantly my dick filled with blood. Not wanting to lose momentum, I reached my hand down my pants and, without pulling it out, started jerking my dick with absolutely no shame. Anyone could have looked at me and assumed I was doing exactly what I was doing, and a minute later, Dafflitto did.

"What the fuck are you doing, sir?" He asked.

"I'm jerking my dick off to stay awake, what the fuck does it look like I'm doing?"

"Jesus, you're really somethin' else."

"You were in fuckin' Sangin mutherfucker! Don't act like you never jerked off to stay awake."

"Oh I absolutely have, many times, but aren't you supposed to be an officer and a gentleman or some shit?"

"Can you shut fuck up? You're DEbonering me right now." I shook my head and looked away, disappointed with his behavior, then turned to look back at him, "as a matter of fact, don't fuckin' look at me, or I'll know for sure you're fuckin' gay."

"Whatever." He looked away.

I continued jerking my dick but was careful not to blow. Had I done that, I would have fallen into a post-sex-coma and would have had to be carried to the bird; so blowing was simply not an option. I felt my stomach growl and remembered how hungry I was. Then I felt a painful thirst for an ice cold, chocolate protein shake. My dream switched from my ex-gf's perfect ass to a protein shake fantasy. I imagined I was back on our small patrol base, sitting on a wooden bench in the gym, in the same position I was sitting in the ditch, and chugging a chocolate protein shake with ice in it. In my dream, my head tilted back as I felt the cold, chocolaty water fill my mouth and slide down my throat. Then I felt it enter my stomach, and I felt my muscles get bigger instantly.

By that point, my daydream had turned into a real dream and I became a hypocritical piece of shit, just two minutes after laughing about how pathetic it was to fall asleep in combat. I fell asleep while sitting up in a ditch, with my hand on my dick, my head tilted back as far as it could go, and waiting to get extracted by helicopters. The entire dream was no more than a few seconds, but it was long enough to make me a piece of shit. All of a sudden I was rocked awake by the sound of a loud explosion to my far right. The sound woke up me out of my doggystyle-protein-shake fantasy as I instinctively lunged forward to the other side of the ditch. I didn't get my hand out of my pants in time, so the weight of my body and the extra 130 pounds I was carrying was absorbed by my left shoulder on the hard dirt. All the wind was knocked out of my body, and I felt like I couldn't get the air back. I looked to my left and right with wide eyes. I knew from the sound it was an

IED. Every Marine who was sitting like I was in the ditch lunged forward at the same time. To my knowledge, I was the only one with my hand down my pants.

My heart was beating out of my chest and my neck was throbbing from the whiplash I had just given myself. I looked around and couldn't see where the explosion was. Everyone had the same look on their face, as we laid on our stomachs in complete silence, awaiting the news that someone else stepped on an IED. The blast sounded far away, but the line of Marines wrapped all the way around the compound wall, so it could have been first platoon. The thought was made more miserable by the fact that first platoon had already lost a good Marine to an IED blast. I hoped with all my heart that the explosion was something other than another one of our Marine's getting his fucking legs blown off. The silence at that moment was miserable, I could hear my heart beating loudly, and without knowing it I held my breath. Every one of us had a knot in our stomach at the thought of another nightmare.

The radio stayed silent, and I waited for the Company Commander to say something, but my impatience didn't let me wait long. I got on my radio.

"All Fox stations, this is Fox Fires, I need a SITREP."

"Fox 1 is good. I see the smoke coming from between two compounds on the other side of the LZ"

"Fox thwee is good," he was Vietnamese and hadn't mastered English yet.

"Sniper 1A is good, I can see the smoke on the other side of the LZ."

"Fox 2 is good."

"Sniper 1B is good."

Finally the Company Commander got on the net and cleared the confusion.

"All Fox stations, this is Fox 6, ICOM traffic says they just blew up their own IED while attempting to front lay us. I think they expect us to head to the compounds on the other side of the LZ."

I made a fist and brought it up to my face in a celebratory "YES!"
I turned to Dafflitto and whispered, "I cannot explain the joy that news brings to my heart. I can just imagine him splattered into a dozen pieces in a walkway. I want to run over and take some pictures, maybe pick up a hand and stuff it in my pack as a war trophy. Think that would be chill?"

"Yeah, you should be good. Just walk across the LZ and ask first platoon and snipers to cover you."

"Don't tempt me boy," I said.

"You won't. You're a pussy."

"Stop it right now."

"Whatever," he paused for effect, "pussy."

We both chuckled.

I couldn't stop smiling at the thought of that piece of shit blowing himself into bits. It seemed like the best way to end the last combat mission of my deployment. Every part of the mission had gone so unbelievably well, that a Taliban shithead blowing himself up right before we got extracted was just
icing on the cake.

A few minutes later, Dafflitto received contact from the pilots and then gave the word, "birds are inbound."

There were four birds inbound, about to pick up the first half of the company. They would drop us off at home, then come back for the second half of the company. It goes without saying, it sucks to be on the second half...

The helicopters were going to land in a specific order, and the crew chiefs were instructed to hold up InfraRed chem lights for us to identify the birds that we were supposed to run to. My squad was supposed to get on the bird that landed second, and had two InfraRed chem lights   hanging   out   the   window.

No matter how many times we did helo missions, it didn't make getting back on the birds any easier, because there was always so much dust created by the helos that we could never see anything. This extract turned   out   to   be   no   different.

The attack helicopters came in first and did a quick recon

and show of force. It was one Cobra and one Huey. They came in low and gave me a hard on as I whispered, " 'MERICA!" to myself. Dafflitto always did the same.

Watching Cobras pass by me at close range and then pull away always seemed like a hot, naked girl was running near me and wanted me to stare at her. I always did, and it should go without saying, it always gave me a hard on.
The attack birds finished their recon of the buildings surrounding the LZ and headed back out to their Battle Position where they would wait for us to load the birds, and would then lead the way home.
My heart rate sped up and I got ready for the worst. There are so many things that can go wrong during a large-scale helo extract, it's impossible not to be worried, and this time I was more than justified.
I laid on my stomach with Dafflitto just a few inches to the left of me. He was talking on the radio to the head pilot and scanning the birds with his NVGs. The four CH-53s moved into their respective positions above the LZ, guided by the IR chem light markings that the snipers made for them.

Just then the Company Commander came on the radio, "All Fox stations, be advised, ICOM traffic says that they are getting into position to attack and will be ready when the helos touch down."
I looked at Dafflitto and shook my head, "This is gonna be the time bro. This is fuckin' it. I knew it had to end. I'll have you know it's been an honor serving with you, Sergeant Dafflitto. I'll be sure to tell your family you died kind of honorably."

"Go fuck yourself."

"You don't mean that."

The company commander came back on the radio, "All Fox stations, be advised, ICOM traffic says they have rockets ready for the attack." This new warning was expected, the Taliban always followed one warning with a more serious warning, because they knew we were listening.

"I know, I don't mean it," Dafflitto said, "It's been pretty cool working with you, sir, not gonna lie."

"Quick kiss?" I said.

"You're the gayest officer in the world."

"You love it."

"I do," he chuckled.

The pilot said something on the radio to Dafflitto. Dafflitto turned to me and said, "Get em up." We turned to the Marines to the left and right of us and yelled, "Get ready to move, pass it on."

The Marines began standing up one at a time, ensuring they had all their gear, and then looked around for the next command. The energy in the air became charged with excitement and seriousness. If anyone was sleeping before, they were wide-awake now, worried that they would be shot at, and even worse, that they'd get lost in the dust on the way to their bird.

The birds all hovered at a few hundred feet and let the dust build up so that the Taliban would have a harder time shooting at them. This was our cue to move. The goal was to time our movement to put us within 50 feet of our bird just as it touched down. This would minimize the time the birds stayed on the ground, because birds were shot at frequently in Shitghanistan. We all waited as the LZ turned into a cloud of dust. Once there was a complete brown out, the birds began descending into the darkness created by their rotor wash.

The leader of my squad was Lieutenant Godfried, the XO. He yelled, "LET'S MOVE, STAY CLOSE." My squad left our position in the ditch and walked into the dust cloud, headed to the piece of ground that our bird was supposed to land on. Once we entered the dust cloud I could barely see. The noise of the four helicopters touching down around us drowned out everything else.
I looked around and saw the silhouettes of the other three squads walking in single file to their helos. I watched the Marines disappear one by one into the dust.

I looked from a squad of Marines, up to my bird, which was slowly descending. I noticed what looked like a power line that I hadn't seen before. I squinted to get a better look. My movement, combined with the dust, the darkness, and my night vision goggles made accurate depth perception and good vision impossible. I raised my NVG's and looked with my naked eye at what I thought was a power line, I looked from the power line to our bird and almost shat my pants, again.

I stopped and turned to Dafflitto, who was behind me, and yelled at the top of my lungs over the roar of the helicopters into his ear, "HE'S GONNA HIT POWER LINES, TELL HIM TO PULL UP!"

Dafflitto yelled back, "WHAT, WHERE?"

I yoked him by the collar and yelled angrily, "TELL HIM RIGHT FUCKING NOW!"

He covered his headset with his hand to shield some of the noise from the helicopters and spoke into the mic. I pointed to the power lines so Dafflitto could see what I saw. We both watched wide-eyed and hoped the pilot would pull up in time. The giant CH-53 continued descending straight towards the power lines at the same speed. If the bird made any contact whatsoever with the power lines, it would go down. Everyone on the bird would, at best, have a few broken bones, and at worst, be dead. Then we would spend the rest of the night and next day holding security for the TRAP team to come pick the bird up.

I was looking forward to beating off and sleeping, so I preferred that the bird to avoid the power lines. I clenched my asshole tight and squealed to myself as I watched the blades of the CH-53 slowly approach the power lines. It looked like a movie scene in slow motion. Just when I thought the blades were going to make contact, the bird missed the power lines by what looked like millimeters. It pulled up and hovered in its initial position, and I relaxed my entire body, including my sphincter, causing shit to drip out of my ass, again.

Since Dafflitto and I stopped, the first half of the squad had continued walking, and by this point were about to disappear into the dust. Dafflitto and I had halted the second half of the squad, splitting us in two. Not wanting to drift too far from the first half of the squad I yelled, "WE GOTTA RUN!" to Dafflitto, and ran to catch up with the rest of the squad.

Dafflitto and I ran up to the front of the squad to talk to Lt. Godfried. He and Dafflitto covered their ears as they talked and listened to the pilot. The squad waited behind us in the dust cloud with worried looks on their faces. I kept looking from Dafflitto, to Godfried, to the bird hovering above us. Finally Dafflitto and Godfried looked at the bird with wide eyes at the same time, which caused me to look at the bird, just in time to see it pull away and take off into the night sky.

We looked at each other in silence as our ride out of Taliban Country flew away. Our eyes were as wide as they could go, Lt. Godfried looked like he was going to shit himself, Dafflitto looked like he was going to vomit, I did shit myself, and in one of the most rare instances in my life, I didn't have a joke; because it was not fucking funny.

Dafflitto looked at me and said, "Oh shit." I couldn't hear him, but I read his lips.
Lt. Godfried yelled, "LOOK!" and pointed behind me.

The other three helicopters were taking off, ascending

out of the dust cloud, and entering the night sky. The loud roar of the helicopter engines quickly faded as the birds disappeared into the stars. There was a very creepy silence as my squad stood out in the middle of an open field, in a thick cloud of dust, with our dicks in our hands. It felt naked, exposed, vulnerable, and flat out weird. Being in the Marine Infantry in a war zone is usually a very powerful feeling, but at that moment, we were a squad of scared little boys.

I knew that helicopters don't travel without their whole wave, but I just watched all four helicopters leave us, so I said as calmly as possible to Dafflitto, "talk to me."

His head was tilted as he listened to the pilot on the radio. He looked back up at me and said, "They're not leaving, they're just getting off the ground so they aren't sitting ducks while they wait for our bird to find a good place   to   land."

"Why doesn't he just land in the same spot that one of the other birds landed?" I asked.
Dafflitto listened for a few seconds, then said, "He is, he's landing in the far one, and he's coming in now so we need to run."

Lt. Godfried reiterated, "He's coming in the far one and he said he's not staying on the ground for long, so we need to fucking run!"
Running in Afghanistan was a nightmare; at night it was worse, and in a cloud of dust was even worse. Not because of IEDs, I mean, those suck too, but because I had the ankles of a disabled 12 year old girl with lupus.

Making matters worse for me, were the extra mortar rounds I still had in my pack, just to prove to the other Lieutenants and Staff Sergeants that I could man-handle more weight than them.

I was literally crushed under the weight of my pack for the entire operation. I felt like a weak little bitch, and a complete fucking moron. As I ran to the bird I resented myself for my childish, ego driven decisions.

Our bird flew over our heads as it headed towards the new LZ position. We had so much weight on our backs that our jog could not have been more than a fast walk without weight. We ran through a thick cloud of smoke that made my NVG's worthless, so I pulled them up and squinted through the dust just to see the Marine in front of me.

The bird touched down a hundred yards in front of us. The crew chief had the ramp down and was waiting outside, clearly in a hurry.

When we got within 20 feet of the bird I turned around to make sure I didn't lose anyone, I saw someone behind me, so I assumed we were good. By this time the dust cloud was thick and the sounds of the rotors drowned everything   out.

As I turned back to the front, I stepped on a rock that must have been strategically placed there by the Taliban. My right ankle rolled right and made a popping sound, then rolled back left and made a louder popping sound. I finally crumbled under the weight of my pack, fell on my face and, thanks to the weight on my back, I couldn't get up.

My ankle felt like Thor had just smashed it with his

hammer, and my whole body went cold for a few seconds. It was an odd feeling. I broke my ankle many times, but this was undoubtedly the worst. One Marine ran right by me on his way to the helicopter, which was disappointing, but being that close to the bird, in the thick dust, it was totally possible that he didn't see me.

The next two Marines grabbed me by my pack and picked me up. I think they were yelling something, but we were so close to the helicopter I couldn't hear anything. I couldn't put any weight on my right ankle, so I unbuckled my waist strap and dropped my pack. It hit the ground hard, and my body went cold again, remembering that I still had three mortar rounds in there. The Marines who were helping me were confused when I dropped my pack, because they just assumed I fell, and didn't realize that I was also crippled.

I grabbed one of my pack straps and dragged my pack on the ground until one of the Marines saw my limp and realized why I was dragging my pack. Both Marines tried to take it but I wouldn't let them, I yoked one of them by the collar and yelled in his ear at the top of my lungs, "GET THE FUCK ON THE BIRD, I GOT THIS SHIT!" The Marines ran the next few feet to the bird, and the crew chief came over to help me. He picked up my pack and carried it while I limped my sorry ass to the last seat on the bird. I don't know why I refused help from my fellow grunts, but happily took help from the air winger...

Once we were on the bird they were done with their head count, and the only Marine they were missing was me. The crew chief gave the pilot a thumbs up and we took off. The bird jolted as the pilot put it into gear and lifted us off the ground. By this point the Taliban had plenty of time to get machine guns and rockets ready, so the knot in my stomach tightened up in anticipation of an attack in midair. Helicopters went down on a weekly basis while I was in Afghanistan, thanks to both sand and enemy fire, so although I was on the bird, I couldn't relax.

I looked out the back door of the bird and watched the Afghan countryside as we flew away. I saw miles upon miles of prehistoric civilization, mud walls, mud houses, and large fields growing all of the world's heroin. I knew I would miss Afghanistan, not because it's a great country (it's a fucking dump), but because it was the only place I ever got to hunt evil human beings. It was the only place I got to live my dream of *doing* what I saw in war movies.

We ascended higher and higher, and eventually I acknowledged that we were out of the Taliban's weapon range. The knot in my stomach finally relaxed, and I let out a loud "URRAH" as a small celebration for extracting with no causalities. That was all the celebration I allowed myself, because for one: we had not landed behind friendly lines yet; two, because the second half of Fox Company was still waiting alone and unafraid out in Taliban Country; and three, I was certain my ankle was broken in several places, again, and I wanted to cry like a bitch.

Our arrival to Forward Operating Base Edinburgh was uneventful. We exited the birds and immediately started searching for all the shit that we probably lost on the op. I saw my old First Sergeant waiting for us proudly as we exited the tarmac of the airfield, and I asked him if he had any word from the second half of our company that was still out there. He said no, but that he'd come back out and tell me if he heard anything.

I postponed my jokes until the second half of the Company got back safely. A few minutes later they did, and at that point I was so giddy I completely forgot I was an   officer.

I began fucking off with Boden as he walked from his bird to our staging area. I held my arms out and yelled from 30 feet away.

"What the fuck, dude? I thought you got shwacked?"

"You wish, bitch," he yelled back.

"Nooooo, I would never wish that on any Marine, but you," I said.

"Yeah well getting killed is a risk when you're leading a rifle platoon in combat you fuckin' fire support pussy."

"Bitch please, your platoon sergeant leads your platoon, you just take credit! Don't be jealous that I rack up more kills than your whole platoon."

At this point he had walked all the way up to me, so I went in to give him a hug, which he usually never accepted from me. I was surprised when he hugged me back, and I should have used that little hug to cement our bond as brothers, but instead I chose to whisper in his ear, "Fuck me," and then kiss his ear. It was really fucking gay, which is exactly why I did it.

He pushed me away and said, "Get the fuck away from me, I will fucking shoot you right now!"
He aimed his weapon at my feet and looked very uncomfortable, as he always did when I got gay with him.

"Dude, you are such a fucking closet homo," I said. "If you just came out you wouldn't have to be so weird man. Don't you know all grunts are gay? I swear to God you're the *only* pretend straight guy in the grunts."

I went back in for another kiss but he jumped back, held up his fist and said, "You are such a fucking fag, Donny, I swear   to   God."

I shook my head in disappointment, "Honestly man, this is how I know your gay. I will accept you no matter what, just be honest with me." I turned to a few Sergeants who happened to be walking by, "Sergeant Dick, are grunts gay?"

He said with a big smile, "The gayest sir," then he grabbed another Sergeant's ass, who returned the favor. They held each other's asses as they walked away. I laughed.

"SEE, Boden! You're the only one!" I said.

"Fuck off O'Malley."

"Whatever nerd, you'll grow up and be gay one day." I left him alone and limped back to my Fire Support Team. "Ok, so what did we lose boys?" I asked with a smile.

Corporal Martinez watched the whole thing between Boden and I. Martinez was the artillery forward observer in my team. He was 6'3", skinny but ripped, looked black but was actually Dominican, was raised by engineers in a WASPY neighborhood in New Hampshire, wore glasses, and was incredibly smart. He said, "Sir, you are one of a kind."

"Why's that, Martinez?"

"Because you relate to enlisted Marines better than any officer I've ever met."

"Lemme' guess, because I pretend to be openly gay, love to fight, hate most officers, and want to fuck and kill everything in sight—dogs, goats, and chickens included?"

"Preeeeee—cisely."

"Well, I take that as a huge compliment devil dog."

"No problem, sir. Oh, by the way, we're just waiting on you to give a thumbs up on all of our personal gear. Aaaaand if you're missing anything sir, just tell me, I got you."

I got excited and pointed at him. "See, this is why I fucking love you, Martinez. Well, that, and you're a fuckin' badass." I walked towards him with my arms open and said, "Get your black ass in here for a hug."

He got uncomfortable and peeked out of the corners of his eyes to see if anyone was looking. He said, "Ummm okay," as I put him in a bear hug.

He looked at me confused, as if he was waiting for me to reassure him, and said, "Sir, you know I'm not black right?"

I waved my hand at him and said, "Yeah, yeah, yeah, black, Dominican, same fuckin' shit. Who gives a fuck?"

"That's fucked up, sir," Martinez said, laughing.

"Oh really?" I turned to Cox, "Hey, Cox, is Martinez black?"

"Black as a spare tire, sir," Cox replied in his Mississippi accent.

I looked at Martinez and pointed to Cox, indicating that he had just validated me.
Martinez shook his head in disappointment, "Still fucked up, sir."

"Look, Martinez, on the outside you may be black, or Dominican, or Caribbean, or whatever the fuck your black ass wants. But on the inside you're green, just like me. That's why you're my brother, and that's why I love you."

"I can dig that, sir," he said smiling.

I looked down at my pack with a worried look on my face. I remembered something that might have been lost, but I didn't know what it was. I thought something fell out of my pocket during one of the many diarrhea shits I had on the Op. After the shit, I didn't do a thorough search of the ground around me because I heard an explosion and ran back to my position. Turned out to be an enemy mortar.

Oh well, shit happens.

Corporal Jeffrey Mount

Job:
0351 Assaultman

Unit:
2nd Battalion, 9th Marines

Battlefields Fought On:
Marjah, Helmand Province, Afghanistan
Sangin, Helmand Province, Afghanistan

Insert: December 24, 1988
Extract: May 26, 2014

Method of Extract:
Self-inflicted GSW to the head

Text a battle buddy,

"I miss you more than I missed my wife on deployment.
No seriously, I wanna cuddle you so hard right now…."

"Ok, ok, so I really want to bang her in the MRAP, is that so fucking bad? I'm showered, I put clean clothes on, I smell great, I shaved for her, not to mention I'm fucking sexy and any woman in her right mind would want me, I have lube and condoms, and I even brought a candle to make it romantic." I pulled out a lighter from my pocket and lit it in front of my face."

When I say I'm gonna do something, I'm gonna fucking do it. If I don't do it, I'm gonna get in a lot of fuckin' trouble or make a big ass of myself as I try.

The Hunt Concludes

2200, July 9, 2012
Porta Potties, FOB Shirgazi, Musa Quala District,
Helmand Province, Afghanistan

When Fox Company returned safe and sound behind friendly lines, we had to spend all day cleaning weapons and gear, doing debriefs, and counting ammo. While my guys were busy working, I interrupted Lance Corporal Cox to get the keys to our MRAP and show me how to unlock the doors. Cox was excited for me to complete my mission and even made some recommendations for positions and placement of both me and my princess in the back of the MRAP. Cox coached me in his Mississippi accent,
"You could put her right up against here, sir, that oughta getchyou a nice angle." He looked around the MRAP for another idea, "Then maybe you could bend her over this chair here, get some nice doggy action goin'. The options

are really endless, sir." I thanked him for his recommendations and assured him that I would give him full credit in a Meritorious Mast or Certificate of Commendation if his sexual positioning schemes worked out in my favor.

We both went back to working for the rest of the day.

By the time Fox Company was done with everything, everyone fell into a deep coma. Everyone but me.

As much as I desired sleep, I desired warm vagina more. I said I was gonna nail the reporter, and I was gonna be goddamned if I didn't give her the opportunity to either have my dick in her, or to respectfully decline my generous offer. Not only was she the most beautiful woman in the entire world, but she was the only woman in the entire world, and I simply couldn't let her go without giving her the chance to tell her friends that she banged Lieutenant O'Malley in a combat zone.

I left my tent after dark and remembered that I had absolutely no idea where she was staying. On my base were two rifle companies, a tank company, an artillery battery, and all the support needed to sustain a FOB. I didn't even know where to begin looking. I realized at that moment that I was taking a shot in the dark at finding a needle in a haystack. All common sense should have dictated that I throw in the towel, throw a beat, and rack the fuck out with a smile on my face, but no, that wasn't good enough for me. I carried on.

I walked to the barracks in the center of base where the Comm Marines lived. I thought I saw the reporter enter one of the buildings before the op, and I knew the barracks there weren't crowded, so I stopped in to see my friend, Sergeant Stanford, the head Comm Marine for our FOB. He was older than me by 5 years, black, and could make anything happen with computers. We were both huge nerds, and we became friends through our mutual love for video games, computer hacking, and sci-fi shit. We nerded-out every now and then in his office.

At the risk of appearing like the creep that I was, I made small talk with him and pretended to be there solely for the sake of hanging out. After half an hour of bullshitting, I had to ask about the reporter,
"Hey, uh, I know this is really random, but do you know where the reporter is? The one from Union Tribune?"

"The blonde one?"

"Yeah, I think it's dirty blonde."

"No, but I thought they put outsiders in the excess tents over by 1st Tanks."

I got excited. I had a possible location for my HVT. "Oh, no shit? Ok, right on."

"Why do you ask, sir?" He had a big suspicious smile on his face. "If I may ask." Stanford was one of the classiest and most polite Marines I knew.

"Oh, no reason, just wanted to say goodbye to her and try to stay in contact."

"Ohhhhh reallllly," he said, nodding his head with it cocked to the side, as if he was pondering the truth in my answer.

"Yeah, is that so hard to believe?" I was pretty sure he knew my intentions.

"Well, anyone else, sir, maybe not, but you, sir, I wouldn't be surprised if you had, how do you say, other motives." He gave me a look that insinuated I wasn't gonna get anywhere with lies.

"Ok, ok, so I really want to bang her in the MRAP, is that so fucking bad? I'm showered, I put clean clothes on, I smell great, I shaved for her, not to mention I'm fucking sexy and any woman in her right mind would want me, I have lube and condoms, and I even brought a candle to make it romantic." I pulled out a lighter from my pocket and lit it in front of my face. Stanford cracked up laughing and almost fell out of his chair.

"Sir, I knew it!! You can't hide from me, sir! I knew it! It's all good, we all have to get ours, sir. But she's hot, so I can see where you're comin' from. I see why you got that fire!"

"RIGHT! I thought she was fucking gorgeous from the moment I saw her. I don't know what everyone else's problem is. Some guys think she's just 'cute.' I think she's fucking drop dead gorgeous."

"They just don't see beauty like you do, sir. You see her true beauty, inside and out."

"Yeah, you mean under and over the clothes right?" We both cracked up. "Because I know she's got a bangin' body under those dorky ass khaki pants." I held my hand up for a high five and he obliged as we both continued laughing like the perverted children that we were.

"Alright, brother, I gotta get going. My love awaits her knight in shining FROG gear."
"Okay, sir, good luck."

I headed out into the night feeling good about myself. Looking back, I always felt good after hanging out with Stanford because he was such a great guy. I truly loved and cherished the friendships I made with Marines.

On my way to 1st Tanks' Company area, I heard gunshots out in the distance, far from base. I smiled knowing that the Afghan's were fighting for their own country without Marine's dying in vain. Little did I know the Taliban were fucking up the Afghan Army so bad the Afghan Army abandoned their post, again.....

I got to 1st Tanks' Company area and realized that I had no idea where to go from there. I did a few laps around their Company area, looking very creepy as I peered in windows while everyone slept. I thought for a second that I would simply open every single door on the fucking base, poke my head in, and ask if anyone had seen the reporter.

Then I thought, *what if someone asks me what I need her for, what do I say?*

No matter how hard I tried, I could not come up with a good answer to that question. I thought maybe I could say, "Oh, I just wanted to give her my contact info." But that would be cheesy. I thought I could also say, "I just wanted to finish our conversation from before the helos picked us up on the op." But since she was guaranteed to be sleeping, that would have sounded a little unnecessary. I concluded that there was simply no way for me to enter and exit my current situation without appearing like the giant creep that I was.

At this point, I should have turned back, but I carried on, knowing that my only chance to get her was to "coincidentally" run into her outside the tents, likely on the way to the bathroom. I planned out and then rehearsed my surprised reaction, utilizing all my experience as an actor, which was really just my last 4 years pretending to be an officer in the Marine Corps.
These were my potential responses and my own critiques. Each one was rehearsed at least 10 times, standing out in the dark with my rifle and my headlamp, in between tents on FOB Shirgazi.

"Oh, Hi, what's goin' on? What're you doin out here? Martha? Right?"
Innocent, surprised, and ignorant.

"Martha, I've been looking all over for you! What's going on?"
Forward, blunt, and creepy.

"Wow, this is a pleasant surprise, I didn't expect to see YOU out here!"
Subtle, surprised, and yet slightly insinuating.

"Martha, hey, how are you? You busy?"
Unassuming, and plain weird.

"Martha, hey, look, I need to be up front with you, there's something I want to show you in the MRAP, it'll be a great story."
Direct, smooth, and just plain honest.

BINGO. That was it.

I walked over to the porta potties, standing about 30 feet away, with a view from all likely avenues of approach, and stood around rehearsing my reaction for at least an hour. After 27 guys with laptops or tablets had entered and exited the porta potties, I thought I'd be well served to do a lap around base. So I did my lap, and as expected, I came up empty.

I returned to my vantage point at the porta potties and sat down on a dirt mound feeling very defeated. I considered throwing in the towel and getting some much needed sleep. I stood up and kicked the dirt like a pouty six-year-old, then laughed at my own patheticness. As I laughed, I tilted my head up and looked at the sky. I took in the beauty of the full Afghan sky and got dizzy, so I looked down quickly and held my arms out to regain my balance. With my balance restored, I looked back up at the stars and took a deep breath in an attempt to fully absorb the beauty of the Helmand Province. I sucked in a huge waft of shit and piss, frowned at the reminder that despite my happiness, I was in a fucking shithole, and then started laughing. I laughed loud and hard as I kept my head tilted back, looking at the stars and almost falling over will laughter. I laughed until my neck hurt and had to look down to release my feeling of vertigo.

As my eyes drifted down I noticed someone walking to the bathrooms. The figure was at least 5' 9", really skinny, with shoulder length blonde hair, wearing civilian khaki pants, and civilian boots.

No way, I thought to myself, *no way.*

I blinked hard and tried to get my mind right as I took another look. Yep, it was her, it was my angel.

Holy fuck, I thought. *This is it, I'm really gonna fuckin' do this, I really am a fucking GOD! ALLAHHUAKBAR!*

I straight up WILLED this into reality. Now there's no way she'll say no. No way. Not after what we survived, and not after our deep and meaningful conversation out in Zamindawar. No way she'll turn me down, I just gotta be blunt, and I can get the pussy. I can get the pussy! I fuckin' got this shit! I'M A GOD! ALLAHHUAKBAR!

My hands started sweating, my dick went from six to twelve, my stomach filled with butterflies and my body even shook a little. My angel came closer, walking through the darkness that was just barely lit by the light of the stars and small crescent moon.

I psyched myself up to ensure that I had the balls to say the last line I had rehearsed. The line that didn't beat around the bush, and the line that I knew would take me to the Promised Land.

When my angel was just 20 feet away I started smiling a big, cheesy, creepy smile. I looked like a little fat kid whose mom was bringing him a giant cake. My mouth opened to say "HI Martha," and I finally got a look at her face. Her hair was way too short. *Maybe she just cut it,* I thought. She walked closer and I noticed her jaw line had gotten a little more defined. *Maybe she's just malnourished,* I thought. She walked a little closer and I noticed that her eyes were more sunk into her head. *Maybe she's just tired,* I thought, desperately holding on to hope.

Then I saw it, plain as day, as if there was a spotlight shining on her face. I saw the face of a skinny, white, dude. It wasn't her, it wasn't my angel, it wasn't my queen, it was a fucking British Spec Ops guy who looked just like her.
I was so fucking horny and desperate that I tried to find the beauty in his face.

This is how I knew I had a serious mental problem, and needed to fix it immediately to avoid court martial, Pattaya flashbacks, and an inability to ever look my father in the eyes again.

It was time to beat off.

Text a bro, and tell him you love him.

After Thoughts and Call to Action

When I think back to my time in combat, I am reminded that my behavior was as primitive as it ever was in my entire life. (And I'm a primitive mutherfucker) This isn't shocking to me, and shouldn't be shocking to anyone, because men in that environment are required to do things that go against human nature. Combat is the most disgusting and primitive scene of humanity, where men go off to become animals, kill and maim each other, laugh about it, and are then expected to return to society as men.

As terrible as I was, I am not ashamed. I'm not proud, but I'm not ashamed; because if I was less disgusting, and less primitive, I might have been a little less willing to mercilessly kill everything I deemed a threat. And as a warrior, that is unacceptable.

For a warrior, killing has to be fun, and when killing is fun, there are a host of other terrible things that will inevitably become fun too. Once a man has gotten to this point, his brain needs a lot of "unfucking" to be normal again.

Consider this for a second-

I sent the reporter this book the second it was finished, for one out of respect, and for two, to fact check our conversation. She responded that she had absolutely NO IDEA that I was even remotely interested in her. Yet, if you reread "The Hunt Continues," you'll notice that in my mind, I was 110% certain that "the pussy was mine." My brain operated in a fantasy land that was only stimulated by sociopathic thoughts of killing and pussy. Like I said, primitive.

Sometimes when I re-read the chapter, "The New York Philharmonic," I shudder in disbelief. A part of me wants to remove it from the book because it is so appalling, but I refuse to tuck the truth away and stuff it in the closet. Those thoughts were real, and I will not deny what I became while I was in combat.

I know there are thousands of men who went to war and thought the same things I did. I hope that reading this lets them know they are not alone, they are not crazy, and they are not subjected to a life as an outcast in society because of what they thought and did in combat.

What they thought and did was NORMAL for a man who was ordered to hunt other human beings, for a man who was ordered to patrol through the same minefield day after day, for a man who watched people close to him get maimed, for a man who lived on the brink of death for months at a time.

There is nothing wrong with us, we are not terrible people, and we are most certainly not the bad guys.

Contrary to what my previous thoughts might allude to, if I actually killed civilians in Afghanistan, I would be a fucking wreck right now, and I too, might be one of the 22. On a previous operation, I thought I killed five civilians by mistake, and immediately my body went cold, I became nauseous, and I began gagging in preparation to puke. That's how I know I'm not a psychopath, and that's how I know I'm one of the good guys. (It turned out to be five Taliban, like I thought)

Americans are the good guys- our brains are wired to do good, to protect people, to stand up to bullies, and kill the bad guys. When we hurt the good people, it hurts our souls and our minds. It twists the wiring in our brains even further, and we become so fucked up and ashamed that we can't communicate nor relate to anyone around us.

I know two guys who killed civilians by mistake and couldn't live with themselves. One guy killed himself, the other couldn't sleep, got addicted to the VA's pills, then became a heroin addict and is now in jail.

Sometimes in war we drop bombs on buildings full of kids by mistake because the Taliban are shooting out of it. Sometimes we shoot a car that we think is full of bad guys, but actually has a family in it. Sometimes we watch kids step on IEDs and get blown to bits right in front of us.

Fucked up shit happens in combat while our minds are already twisted, and when we hurt good people, it fucks our minds so badly we hate ourselves, and some of us would rather die by our own hand than live with that self-hate.

Like I said at the beginning of this book, my experience was **weak** compared to what many other guys have experienced. Think about the WW2, Korea, and Vietnam guys, Fallujah, Ramadi, and Sangin guys. If I was *that* disgusting, imagine what *they* were like while in combat. I hope my book inspires them to write their honest memoirs. The more guys who come out with the raw, honest, truth that the public doesn't want to know, the fewer guys we might have killing themselves- because we'll all know we're not alone in our thoughts, and that's important.

My only regret is not writing this book sooner.

For the few civilians who had the balls to read this book, first, I applaud you. Second, I hope this honest insight into the mind of a grunt in combat leads you to be a bit more compassionate when you see some military guys acting like psychopaths at the bar. Please let them be, give them space, and politely ask them to leave when they've gone too far. Their brains are not right, please forgive them.

Call to Action

I want this book to bring guys together. I want this book to be responsible for motivating combat veterans to ACTIVELY REACH OUT to their brothers, and continue to be a good squad or team leader. Take care of your bros. Call and text them frequently, identify who's at risk for suicide, set up events, trips, bar crawls, or anything that gets the guys together. Suicide is now just more common as being KIA, and almost as common as getting cancer. EVERYONE knows *someone* who has committed suicide, and unfortunately for all the grunts, we know LOTS of guys who have committed suicide.

The next thing I want combat vets to do is to get involved with the VFW. These posts have great locations, great prices on drinks and food, good people, and one huge problem. NO FUCKING MEMBERS!

Why? I can only assume that it's because the membership is mostly older vets (Nam, Korea, and WW2 guys), who don't understand how fucking gay and weird the younger generations of warriors are. (I don't know why but I'm positive that we're more gay than warriors used to be)

Some of the older breed attempts to maintain a sense of professionalism and honor when speaking about their service. They uphold the image that the public wants to keep of our military, and of war, but it's a load of bullshit, and my generation wants nothing to do with it.

Many guys in my generation prefer to make a joke about everything we did. We tell war stories with a smile and laughter.

Much like the Vietnam guys, my generation is stuck knowing that everything we did in the sandbox was for nothing. Every ounce of effort we put into training the Iraqi and Afghan Army was a waste. Every senior officer who proudly told his boss that his area was "ready for turnover to the native people," was wrong.

We can be angry about it, we can cry about it, we can bitch about how stupid everything was; or we can make a joke about it. I choose to joke, that's how I cope, and that's how many of my friends cope. I acknowledge that the jokes aren't for everyone, and I ask that those who don't like the jokes, understand the irreverent humor is simply a coping mechanism, and let us cope the way we choose.

Some will cry, I will laugh.

Back to the VFW- if ALL of us sign up for the VFW membership and join a post, we will make it OUR organization, and when the old-timers kick the bucket, WE will step up to run it. There is really no excuse for not joining the VFW—it's one of the last, best, and most patriotic organizations in the United States.

Our local VFW needs to become our new frat house/barracks, and when the old guys die, we will step up to run the place and give it the makeover that it desperately needs.

My first Company Gunny reminded me that no one will ever understand what we've been through who hasn't been there. **No one can help a veteran who has done and seen terrible things, unless they've done and seen those terrible things themselves**. Counselors and therapists can call veterans all day long, they can sit and meet with us, they can say "WE'RE HERE FOR YOU!" until they're blue in the face, but the sad reality is that no matter how hard that counselor tries, he's not going to get through to that veteran, because the only thing going through that veteran's mind is,

"How fucking dare you try to make me feel better about what I've done? Who the fuck do you think you are? What gives you the fucking nerve to think you can help me? How many friends did you watch die? How many people have you killed? How many times did you wake up with your hands around your wife's neck? When the fuck did you ever sleep walk in the middle of the night and throw your own child down the fucking stairs? YOU DON"T FUCKING UNDERSTAND ME, CUZ YOU HAVEN'T FUCKING BEEN THERE!"

It's sad, because these good-hearted Americans want to help veterans, but unless they've been to combat, they usually can't.

That means it's up to US. As combat veterans, we have to help ourselves. It needs to start with organization. Active duty units have never done much for veterans, they have to focus on the mission ahead of them, so that means the alumni of every unit need to step up and create a way for their brothers to communicate to each other.

It should start with a simple Facebook Page, a website if possible, and a closed Facebook group.

If there are better methods available, I'd love to hear them, but Facebook at the moment is free and easy.

Next, every single battalion in the Marine Corps has a unit website. If the Marine Corps really wants to stop this suicide trend as they claim in the press, the LEAST they could do is add an "ALUMNI" tab to each unit's page to help facilitate communication amongst veterans of the same unit. The alumni tab could then be divided into dates/deployments, and then into Companies, and then into platoons. It's not good enough to have a 2/5 Facebook Page, because every deployment has a completely different experience that is best understood by those who were there. Therefore each Facebook Page should be specific to the year and deployment.

Under the 2/5 "Alumni" tab, the list will look like this:

31st MEU- 2014- Click here to go to the Official Facebook page.

Musa Quala/Now Zad- 2012- Click here to go to the Official Facebook page.

31st MEU- 2011- Click here to go to the Official Facebook page.

Garmshir/Lashkar Gah/Marjah- 2010- Click here to go to the Official Facebook page.

15th MEU- 2009- Click here to go to the Official Facebook page.

and so on...

Each Company and Platoon could have their own OFFICIAL page and group, that is deemed official by the Marine Corps.

The only way it will ever get done is if Marine Corps leadership slaps their hand on the table and makes this a fucking order.
That's what I want this book to create, aside from laughter induced defecation and violent masturbation: a Marine Corps fucking ORDER that proves they are committed to reducing post war KIAs.

The same can be done for Army Units, Rangers, SEALs, PJs, and everyone else who feels they need it. I come off as pretty exclusionary by only focusing on infantry type units, but the reality is that even aircraft mechanics, like my good friend, can get a little fucked up in the head when every other week in combat, a new friend gets killed by a perfectly placed enemy mortar round in the middle of the night. I can't relate to his experience, only guys from his unit can, and therefore, guys from his old unit need to get together and support each other.

Let's sum up my call to action.

1. Reach out to your old combat brothers/sisters, and do it often. It could literally save a life.

2. Join the VFW, get ALL your buddies to join the VFW, and start throwing parties/dinners/events there that get the guys together in celebration of the fact that we're still alive.

3. For our Congressional and Marine Corps Leadership- understand and accept the fact that the best way to decrease the suicide rate is to <u>facilitate the communication amongst combat veterans of the SAME UNIT, and the same BATTLEFIELD.</u>
So don't make me micromanage you, you've had the commanders intent (stop vet suicide) for a while now and haven't been effective. Now you have the mission, (facilitate communication amongst Marines/soldiers of the same unit/battlefield) so figure it the fuck out.

4. Every now and then, sit around with a few battle buddies and talk about whatever the fuck is eating you up inside. Talk about the kid you nailed by mistake, talk about the time you watched your bro take one to the head, talk about the time you had to tourniquet your buddies legs and he still ended up dying, talk about your buddies body parts that you had to stuff into your backpack or cargo pockets, talk about the bomb that landed on a bus full of civilians.

We've all done and seen fucked up shit; that's the nature of war, and always will be. **If you don't talk about it, it'll eat at you forever until it fucking kills you**.

Let those mother-fucking demons out. This is the only way you'll ever feel better about what you've done and seen.

Demons don't go away without an exorcism.

When you get three buddies together, go camping for a night in the middle of nowhere, and let all your demons out of your soul, that's exactly what you're doing. You're having an exorcism.
Exorcise the demons.

5. Step up like a squad leader, and get vets together. Get together, talk, and go from there.

This book serves as my letter to the Commandant, and my letter to Congress. If they are as serious about helping vets as they say they are, they WILL make a change, and they WILL facilitate communication amongst veterans of the same unit and battlefield.
I'm not a religious man, but right now, I have faith.

Love and kisses,

"Donny O'Malley," Captain, USMC, (ret)

IRREVERENT WARRIORS™
Healing with Humor

This book is just the beginning of a life long career of entertaining veterans and bringing them together. I have created a community of combat vets called

Irreverent Warriors starting with my group of friends, that has now exploded all over the country into a large non-profit organization.
www.irreverentwarriors.com

We are a California non-profit and have 501(c)(3) tax status.

Mission:
We bring veterans together using humor and camaraderie to heal the mental wounds of war, through therapeutic events and entertainment, in order to reduce PTSD and prevent veteran suicide.

We have a process to get vets to stop with the pills, put the gun back on the nightstand, and never consider putting it to their heads again.
1) A veteran comes to one of our events and watches/reads our entertainment.
2) That veteran connects with other vets who are going through similar struggles.
3) All veterans connect with the host of resources and veteran support organizations that we are partnered with.
4) Each veteran improves the quality of their life with jobs, support, veteran service organizations, and therapy.
5) With improved esteem and outlook on life, the veteran puts the gun back in the drawer, and never thinks about putting it to his head again.

We have several YouTube shows planned and created that will serve as therapy for combat veterans.

The YouTube channel will feature several shows, "Irreverent War Stories," "Kill, Die, Laugh," "Irreverent Update," and more. All full of dark military humor intended to help combat vets laugh at the things that might be eating them up inside.

All money made from my books, audiobooks, comics, and events will be spent on creating more comedy. If you want to be part of the military humor production, please contact me.

My goal is to staff my production company with 100% combat veterans. This includes production assistants, accountants, lawyers, actors, directors, photographers, writers, graphic editors, video editors, sound engineers, runners, everyone.

I'm also working on a mobile application and a search engine that will have the ability to search by "BATTLEFIELD."
As far as I've seen, guys who fought on the same battlefield have an instant connection. So if my goal is to connect veterans to each other so that we can support each other, searching by "Battlefields Fought On" might not be a bad start. It can't hurt to try.
Our non-profit needs volunteers with skillsets, if you want to be involved, please email us through the website.

BTW- The 22 a day statistic is fucking WRONG. That number doesn't include stats from 29 states. The real number is probably well over 40.

ACKNOWLEDGEMENTS

The first thanks goes to every one who volunteered in a time of war. That took balls. Special shout out goes to all grunts and operators, who accepted and over came challenges that few men in the history of the world have stepped up to. I need to give special love to all the POG's who work long hours, doing shitty, thankless jobs, and then get pissed on by the arrogant grunts. I thank you from the bottom of my heart for all your hard work. Despite some of my obnoxious jokes, I really do love and appreciate all of you. (Minus a handful of worthless admin dickheads who are just plain pieces of shit who I hope hit an IED on the way to work tomorrow)

To all the good ole' boys I served with in Echo and Fox 2/5, you guys are my heroes.

Of course, I could never have done anything in life, let alone write this book, without the love and support from my incredible family. Mom, Dad, Jason, Grandma, and the large group of lifelong friends who I consider my family. (I'm blessed with a lot of friends, I mean, really blessed.) As odd as it sounds to thank my mother for supporting me as I wrote a book as vile and disgusting as this, I must. Mom always knew that deep down, her piggish son has a soft heart and good intentions.

Throughout the writing process I put my friends and family through a ton of garbage, half-ass stories that were probably painful to read, so I thank you all for reading them.

I have a special thank you reserved to my good friend Dan Ottinger, a Marine officer I met in booty camp, went through school with, and lived with in San Clemente while we were grunt lieutenants. Dan is a fucking nut, a hermit, a hobbit, a comedic genius, a sloth, a supportive friend, and a fucking weirdo. When I first began writing, I sent Dan a couple of my stories and asked him to critique them. He ripped them apart worse than anyone has ever ripped up my writing. He told me it was "despicable, pathetic, shit." Within 2 hours I was enrolled in a writing class at UCSD, and two more classes soon after. Without his loving and constructive critique, my writing would still be at a 5th grade level. (I'm only at 7th grade now)

I must also thank all my friends and family for the support I received while I was in combat, you all made the experience much better. A special thank you must go to my ex-gf, who shall remain anonymous. She was my number one supporter while I was in combat, at my beck-and-call every day, despite the fact that I broke up with her before I left. (She was ready for a lifelong commitment and I was clearly not.) I'll never forget how much unconditional love, support, and happiness she gave me every day. For that I will always love her.

A big thank you must given to Alyssa, who pushed me more than anyone else in my life to connect with my Marine audience, and write this book immediately. Everyone supported me, but she *pushed* me to write my military stories. For that I'll always love her.

Mom and Dad, don't worry, this book will do so much good that you're friends won't judge you for my disgusting mouth/thoughts/actions.

ONE LAST THING ABOUT ME.......

In the last year that I've had my stories posted on my website I have been on numerous occasions, compared to the young Tucker Max.

I want to get something straight, while some aspects of our humor are similar, there is one glaring difference between the young Tucker and I.

If I ever saw him call a girl "fat" in my presence I would have knocked him unconscious, waited for him to wake up, then made him apologize to her. If he refused to apologize, his medical bill would have been as painful as his face.

While I did laugh at some of his humor, there were at least three dozen times in the hundred or so pages I read of his book when he was blatantly *mean* to other people and I thought to myself, *"oh my God I would have fucking hospitalized him if I saw him do that."*

I cannot speak for the man he is now, but back then Tucker branded himself an "asshole" and made it seem cool to insult people and be mean.

I think its cool to be NICE to people. Yes, I make terrible jokes, but I brand myself a kind, caring, and loving guy with a horrible sense of humor, who likes to make people feel good, loves killing the enemies of the United States, who would happily die in battle or while protecting his brother, and also happens to love warm vagina. (Who doesn't?)

So yeah, please don't confuse me with Tucker Max. I'll be speaking all over the U.S. at military bases, VFW's, and colleges. My speeches are partly inspiring, partly disgusting, partly educational, and mostly stand up comedy.

Text a bro right now,

"Wanna have a threesome with my wife? She fucked the neighbor so she owes me a solid......"

We'll meet soon. Stand the fuck by to stand the fuck by.

Oh, and since you're my bro I gotta' tell you, "O'Malley" isn't my real last name.

When I first joined the Marines I changed my name on Facebook and made another account under my real name so that I could keep my job. Had my superiors seen my original Facebook, and the thousands of pictures of me at my theme parties dressed in anything from a baby in a diaper to my alter ego, Donna, they would have undoubtedly kicked me out of the Officer Corps. A friend of mine gave me the nickname Donny O'Malley, (at a 1920's theme party) and it stuck. When it came time to make my website I was still active duty, so I *had* to use a pseudonym. Since then I've realized that my pseudonym sounds exactly like what you'd expect when you meet me. A jolly, loving, witty, heavy drinking, loud-laughing guy who's gonna grab your ass and tell you you're gay if you don't like it.

Despite what you might assume, I was actually raised really well by two very loving and professional parents, and I didn't want to ruin the family name, just yet. If I meet you in person, one-on-one, I'll be using my real name, but on stage, it's O'Malley.

Later bro. xoxoxo

LETTER TO MARINE CORPS LEADERSHIP,

I have always been under the impression that the Marine Corps did not have the time to pay attention to anything other than the "live rounds" who were ready to deploy. However, considering the current suicide rate, considering the Marine Corps "awakening" (that was apparently sleeping while gunshots were being fired into veteran's heads), and considering the verbal commitment made by the Commandant to fight veteran suicide; it only seems fitting to demand that the Corps take action. This plan is from my first Company Gunny, who was one of my greatest mentors as a new Lieutenant, new Captain, and now, newly retired combat veteran's advocate.

An edited note from Dave Boire, Gunnery Sergeant, USMC, (ret)

For 13 years I watched the Marine Corps spend millions of dollars and thousands of hours taking care of, catering to, and bending over backwards for dependents and spouses. This is without a doubt necessary; however, never once in my career did I hear a unit talk about getting the unit's veterans together, thanking them, supporting them, nor showing their appreciation for them.

Every unit is proudly wearing colors, ribbons, and medals that were earned by the *veterans* of that unit. Meaning everything a unit has to be proud of, was done by men who came before them. We must honor these men by taking care of them and supporting them, not just thanking them.

While the people of the United States have been supportive of our combat veterans, the only people that combat veterans can relate to, and are influenced by, are other combat veterans. Unfortunately, the units that each veteran has served with have not shown much interest in supporting the very men who made that unit great.

Many years ago the Marine Corps decided that giving more attention to the families of Marines was imperative to mission readiness. As a result the Marine Corps created the FRO, (Family Readiness Officer) to do exactly that, and many FRO's have done a good job taking care of the families.

Now that combat veterans are blowing their brains out at the sustained rate of at least 22 a day, (the actual number is much higher than that) it's time the Corps puts their money where their mouth is, and actually do something about their combat veterans by hiring someone to care for them; a Combat Veteran Advocate.

The Combat Veteran Advocate position is a pilot program that should be implemented in two Infantry Regiments; 5th Marines and 1st Marines.
Why just there?

For one, because many of the suicides are by Infantry types who went to combat. **We can't save everyone**, and we have to start somewhere, so we might as well start with the front line warriors who had to kill the enemy and watch their brothers get maimed.

Two, because both Regiments are in Camp Pendleton, which is surrounded by veterans and opportunities to the north and south.

Each Infantry Battalion would get one UVA, paid $40,000 a year, making the yearly cost of the UVA position for the trial program $280,000. Add a $5,000 budget for each Battalion, and the total cost of this pilot program is $315,000. The U.S. military spends more than this on much less important things, every day.

The salary is low, yes- but this job is intended to be filled by a combat veteran of the same unit who is doing it with noble intentions.

The Marine Corps values a human life at $400,000 (SGLI payout), so if the program saves one life, it was well worth the money.

-Combat Veteran Advocate-

Job Description:

-Track as many veterans as possible. Of those who will allow or give permission to stay in contact, the CVA creates and maintains a database of them.

-Rate those veterans.

> 1-Doing fine
>
> 2- Doing OK, but could benefit from regular contact/check-ins
>
> 3- Needs help
> 3a- VA problems
> 3b- Financial problems
> 3c- Benefits problems
> 3d- Employment help
>
> 4- Failing to adapt
>
> 5 - ALERT STATUS- Suicidal, homicidal.

-Create a network for employment opportunities. (There are so many out there that no one knows more than 10% of the opportunities)

-Knowledgeable in VA Educational benefits, claims and Advocacy. Maintain a network of connections with VSO (Veteran Service Organization) procedures and VA procedures.

-Create a network with civilian veterans organizations that offer therapeutic getaways and life improving courses.

-Create a unit fund for veterans' functions. At least one unit reunion per year.

-Create a network within the units' veterans who are doing well financially- to maintain a fund that brings selected Marines back to their Unit's HQ for Veteran Appreciation Days/Weekends; especially for those veterans who have been rated 4 or 5.

-Establish and Maintain relationships with VSO's from DAV (Disabled American Veterans)

-Establish and Maintain a Unit Veteran webpage where all veteran programs and knowledge is located. Make the webpage track what members are viewing in order to further facilitate their needs.

-Establish and maintain assistant regional advocates (volunteer positions) they will plan quarterly veteran events in their region

---

I implore the Marine Corps to modify this plan, put it into action, and supervise it- or don't ever claim to be "doing everything we can to stop veteran suicide."

If the pilot is effective, we keep it and expand to other Infantry Battalions. If it's not, it gets modified or scratched; but it can't hurt to try.

We operate on a 70% solution, and I just handed you an 80% solution. It's time to take action gentlemen.

ABOUT THE AUTHOR

Donny O'Malley should be an award-winning actor for his six year performance as an Infantry Officer in the play, "Marine Corps," which has been running since 1775. Donny was injured on set and was medically retired. He now lives in a sunroom in a senior citizen community in San Diego where he takes care of his grandma. His latest acting gig is a role as the founder and president of a large non-profit for veterans in the show titled, "Irreverent Warriors," which can be seen on YouTube. Donny kindly asks that you don't kill yourself until you've read all his writing and watched all his videos. If you still have the urge to pull the trigger, please leave a suicide note that includes the verbiage, "Donny you failed me," or something to that effect.

You can find him on Facebook, Instagram, Twitter, and his website,
www.donnyomalley.com

BOLO for new books by Donny O'Malley

"My Roomie and Me"

Donny moves in to take care of his Grandma, the most lovingly bigoted and patriotic Grandma in America. Donny soon learns that grandpa is an abusive bastard, and kicks him out of the house. Grandma begins a new life without the old man's BS, and a beautiful friendship is formed, all the while giving Donny lessons on sex, race, gays, and frugality.

"Embarrassing Confessions of a Convenient Humanitarian"

Donny travels to Africa to climb Mt. Kilimanjaro, scuba dive in Zanzibar, volunteer in an orphanage, and hug black babies while avoiding Ebola. He discovers Africans are way cooler than blacks in Ferguson, he wants to adopt an African baby, and that he has a soft spot for the whole filthy continent.

And more to come….

To follow Donny's adventures running a large non-profit, creating a comedy show, public speaking, traveling the world, throwing raging parties, and of course, taking care of his lovably racist Grandma, go to-

www.donnyomalley.com/blog